KIDS,
SEX &
SCREENS

KIDS, SEX & SCREENS

Raising Strong, Resilient Kids in the Sexualized Digital Age

Jillian Roberts, Ph.D.

Brimming with creative inspiration, how-to projects, and useful information to enrich your everyday life, Quarto Knows is a favorite destination for those pursuing their interests and passions. Visit our site and dig deeper with our books into your area of interest: Quarto Creates, Quarto Cooks, Quarto Homes, Quarto Lives, Quarto Drives, Quarto Explores, Quarto Gifts, or Quarto Kids.

First Published in 2019 by Fair Winds Press, an imprint of The Quarto Group, 100 Cummings Center, Suite 265-D, Beverly, MA 01915, USA.
T (978) 282-9590 F (978) 283-2742 QuartoKnows.com

Fair Winds Press titles are also available at discount for retail, wholesale, promotional, and bulk purchase. For details, contact the Special Sales Manager by email at specialsales@quarto.com or by mail at The Quarto Group, Attn: Special Sales Manager, 100 Cummings Center, Suite 265-D, Beverly, MA 01915, USA.

22 21 20 19   1 2 3 4 5

ISBN: 978-1-59233-852-8

Digital edition published in 2019
eISBN: 978-1-63159-567-7

Library of Congress Cataloging-in-Publication Data
Names: Roberts, Jillian, 1971- author.
Title: Kids, sex & screens : raising strong, resilient children in the
  sexualized digital age / Jillian Roberts.
Other titles: Kids, sex and screens
Description: Beverly, MA : Fair Winds Press, 2019. | Includes index.
Identifiers: LCCN 2018033138 | ISBN 9781592338528 (trade pbk.)
Subjects: LCSH: Children and sex. | Internet and children. | Parenting.
Classification: LCC HQ784.S45 R63 2019 | DDC 004.67/8083--dc23 LC record available at
https://lccn.loc.gov/2018033138

Cover Image: gettyimages
Cover Illustration: FamilySparks
Illustrations: Colleen Frakes
Page Layout: Sporto
Design: Sporto

Printed in USA

To protect the privacy of those involved, names and identifying information have been changed.

Certified Chain of Custody
Promoting Sustainable Forestry
www.sfiprogram.org
SFI-01268

SFI label applies to the text stock

I dedicate this book to Marie.
Je t'aime, Maman.

CONTENTS

INTRODUCTION

Our kids today are seeing more sexualized content, accessed unfiltered from more screens, than ever before. There's a tsunami of explicit photos, videos, and sexts just off the coast of your child's brain, ready to come crashing in. And all this content now fits right inside your kid's pocket.

You've probably heard horror stories: the child who stumbles onto porn while researching a science project; one who is pressured to engage in sexual acts by peers; or one who sends or receives a naked photo on social media. We all want to prevent these kinds of scenarios, but we can't put our kids in a bubble. So what can parents do?

I've been guiding parents and children for years on the subject of sex and, unfortunately, the horror stories I just mentioned are real-world examples that come up during counseling sessions in my child psychology practice and in my company, FamilySparks.com. The past five years have brought more changes regarding sex than any other period of my professional career—I now regularly see kids stumbling onto

pornography, participating in sexting, engaging in or being victimized by sexualized bullying, and feeling confused about what consent means.

Kids, Sex & Screens shows parents how to throw a life preserver to their sons and daughters. Our kids are being exposed to a great deal of sexualized content, and we don't want to put our heads in the sand but rather deal with that reality in a proactive, thoughtful way. In this book, you'll learn crucial navigational tools to help keep your children safe amid these turbulent seas. Raising strong, resilient kids isn't easy in the digital age, but I'll help you through it.

"The Talk" is no longer a one-time conversation about the birds and the bees. By necessity, it's evolved to become a series of ongoing discussions, tips, and examples offered to kids throughout the years. It *must* be accompanied by "The Other Talk" as well, the one where you acquaint kids with the online world and draw a path of safety through the myriad pitfalls that await.

SEVEN POINT Parental Compass

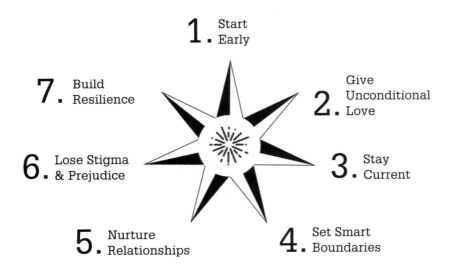

1. Start Early

7. Build Resilience

2. Give Unconditional Love

6. Lose Stigma & Prejudice

3. Stay Current

5. Nurture Relationships

4. Set Smart Boundaries

My goal is to help you build an open relationship with your kids, so that instead of Googling a question about their bodies or sexual content, they'll be more likely to come to you. The alternative is that they search a topic online and think, "OMG, so that's what that looks like—no wonder nobody wants to talk to me about it." Unfortunately, this happens too often, and can have some deep psychological effects, including a skewed understanding of what a healthy sexual relationship looks like, a distorted perception of consent, and a fractured parent-child relationship.

We'll begin with an overview of the new reality our daughters and sons are living in, nearly all of which is different from the landscape in which we grew up. I'll share with you some important information about how coming of age has changed for our children. I'll then go over how the very definitions of sex have changed for this generation and talk about the effects of social media that complicate everything. The context of sex in your child's development is extraordinarily different from its role in your own growing-up years. Many kids are learning about sex or seeing sex for the first time online, either from or in the company of peers. Parents should talk with their children about how mistakes on social media, often regarding issues of sex, can follow both boys and girls into adulthood, and I'll share some examples from my practice that illustrate the dangers.

Kids, Sex & Screens does something that no other parenting book on this subject does: explain how to protect your child but *also* what to do if something difficult or damaging occurs. I'll introduce you to the Parental Compass, a tool that gives you the know-how—and the confidence—to prevent and combat the effect of the images, media portrayals, and peer expectations your children are confronting every day.

Each point on the Compass lines up with a parenting practice that enriches the parent-child bond and builds resilience, which will equip your child to handle the increasingly complex pressures she faces in today's world. Individually, these practices may seem relatively simple, but don't let that simplicity fool you. Taken together, the Compass points are powerful and will ensure that neither you nor your children get lost in the storm of sexual content directed at your kids. We'll look at each of these points, including the psychology behind them and how they're all connected.

Throughout the book, we'll delve into the psychological effects that today's hypersexualized atmosphere can have on kids, illustrated by stories from my clinical practice that center around bullying on social media, video game addiction, casual sex at an early age, and more. Please know that, though these stories are based on real people I have seen in my practice, they are composites of many cases rolled into one example. Names and identifying details have been changed throughout

to protect patient privacy. Although the cases may be extreme, they are not far removed from normal childhood experience, and what happened to these kids could happen to any child.

My Parental Compass is essential when you're facing difficult problems such as the ones encountered by my patients and their families, but it's also essential to prevent these kinds of situations from occurring in the first place. Throughout *Kids, Sex & Screens*, you'll find the knowledge and insight you'll need to raise strong, resilient kids in our highly sexualized digital age. Parents of both boys and girls need to understand the range of content and situations their children might be exposed to, how that experience can affect kids psychologically, and the strategies parents can use to help their families in these critical moments.

I've spent my career—in my counseling practice, as a university professor, and through FamilySparks.com—helping parents not only survive challenges but thrive as they move past them. This book offers a crash course on the principles I've imparted to the thousands of families I have worked with during the past two decades. Times have changed, for sure, and the forces aligned in front of our kids can seem insurmountable, but together we'll take it one step at a time. *Kids, Sex & Screens* provides the map you need to navigate safe passage for your child through adolescence and beyond.

Let's get started.

CHAPTER 1

NAVIGATING WITH THE PARENTAL COMPASS

Long gone are the days when children learned about the birds and the bees from their parents in an awkward conversation. Even the images a kid saw when he found his older brother's *Playboy* stash are tame compared with what kids are likely to see when they stumble onto sexual content today. In the past, a child who witnessed the act of intercourse had probably accidentally walked in on parents in the bedroom or clicked on the wrong cable channel late at night. Now kids often learn about sex in the company of friends or peers, often online. Sometimes they witness situations or acts that represent sex in an extreme form, such as scenes involving group sex, bondage, and/or questionable consent (e.g., depictions of violence, domination, or abuse).

My office is inundated with calls about children who have been traumatized after stumbling onto pornography, being taken advantage of via sexting, or being otherwise exposed to mature content. On the other end of the phone line are parents worried about the ramifications of their kids seeing things such as bondage and violent group sex online. Young girls are frightened that this is what will soon be expected from them. Some kids wonder whether this is how they were conceived. They think maybe this is why adults are so embarrassed to talk about sex.

None of this is a healthy introduction to sexuality.

Drastic Differences

Given the variety of electronic devices that even young children wield with expertise and the wide access to material the Internet provides, there is no doubt that today's parenting landscape looks drastically different from the one our parents inhabited. Our society has changed in meaningful ways, many of them attributable to the digital transformation we've undergone; over a short period of time, technology has dramatically changed the way we communicate and access information. Kids carry around in their pockets a portal to the entire world. There are many benefits to this access, as kids can learn about anything they are interested in, connect with people across the globe, and see with their own eyes, in real time, events that are important to all of humanity. When the information isn't filtered (or when a filter fails), however, the underbelly of this world can slink into their pocket, usurp their attention, and prey on their psyches.

Although sex ed continues to be taught in classrooms throughout North America (curricula vary from region to region), the lessons still focus mostly on biology, leaving the crucial matter of context up to parents. A good first step is to check in with your child's school and learn about the programs they have in place. Review any materials your child brings home. This will help you identify gaps that you need to fill by educating your kids within your family.

Often the emotional and psychological aspects of sex are left out of school programs, but those are just as important as the physical facts. No two families are alike, and we all have different beliefs about how, when, and why to have conversations about sex with our kids—so make the decisions that best align with your personal values, keeping in mind that your kids will benefit from hearing from you before they learn about sex from friends or other sources. Please see the resources at the end of this book.

Many in the generation educating kids today—both parents and teachers—feel ill-equipped to help children navigate the obstacles they face. These parents and other adults may find themselves having to tackle sexually charged situations they never could have imagined and figure out technology or social media platforms they may not fully understand. I have had many mothers disclose to me that they have only ever laid eyes on pornographic magazines, and that they have never actually seen pornographic videos. How do they even begin to help their kids process what they see? This is a specific type of generation gap, the likes of which we've never seen before.

Parents today may have been shamed about sexuality when they were growing up or given the message that sex is a taboo subject. Whether or not that was the case for you, you cannot bring that attitude into your relationship with your own child. We no longer have the time or space for shame around the subject of sex. The changes that have taken place in our culture require that our children (from elementary school age to the tween and teen years) know they can share their thoughts and experiences with their parents without being shamed.

We need to accept the fact that we live in arguably the most sexualized landscape in human history. As parents, we must push past any taboos that may have been ingrained in us and any embarrassment we may feel to position ourselves as the go-to people our kids can talk to about this complicated topic. Figuring it all out is hard enough for adults; just imagine what it's like for our children!

By the Numbers

It's one thing to feel that the world has changed, but it's another to look at the actual statistics. Although various studies produce slightly different results, depending upon methodology and the demographics of the sample, it's clear that many kids are coming into contact with mature content. Here are some facts that every parent should be aware of:

- According to a 2013 published study in the *Journal of Sex Research*, the average age of exposure to pornographic content for boys was eleven and the average for girls was thirteen.
- By age fifteen to sixteen, 65 percent of teens reported having seen pornography, based on a study from 2016 out of Middlesex University in London.
- In looking at risks and safety on the Internet, one in five European children said in 2011 that they have seen obviously sexual images in the past twelve months, whether online or offline.
- According to a 2008 study in New Hampshire titled "The Nature and Dynamics of Internet Pornography Exposure for Youth" and published in *CyberPsychology & Behavior*, 73 percent of teen participants (93 percent of boys, 62 percent of girls) had seen online pornography before age eighteen.
- That same study reported that most exposure began when the youths were ages fourteen to seventeen, and boys were significantly more likely to view online pornography more often and view more types of images than girls.

As a psychologist who works with children and adolescents, I am not surprised by these statistics. In my clinical practice, I have dealt time and again with situations that underline this reality. However, in recent years I have become increasingly alarmed as I observe the ages of the children affected creeping lower and lower. It is not unusual for me to see pre-teens deeply troubled and confused by explicit content they see online or sexually charged stories they hear from their friends and classmates.

When I talk with these young people, they explain that they understand the mechanics of sex and how babies are made and born, but they have no idea (and have no real interest yet) about what actually happens in the bedroom. One curious kid in one unsupervised session on any kind of device can uncover a never-ending trove of videos that confuse her understanding of human sexuality. Kids rarely keep such shocking discoveries to themselves. Indeed, they often share the information eagerly with other kids, and the ripple effect begins. It's too much, too soon.

A child doesn't need to be exposed to porn to experience the negative effects of our hypersexualized world. Sending or receiving naked photos, soliciting or being solicited for sexual acts, and being involved in sexualized bullying are more common than most parents know. Sexting—having a sexual conversation via text, sometimes with the exchange of personal photos—is also prevalent, and not just among older teens. As shocking as it might be to imagine, children as young as ten or eleven know about sexting, and some are even participants.

Nearly half of high school boys and more than 30 percent of high school girls reported having received a sext, with nearly 20 percent of both genders reporting having sent a sext of themselves, according to a 2013 study published in *Archives of Sexual Behavior*. A 2017 study published in the *Journal of American Medical Association Pediatrics* states that approximately one in eight young people reports that they have either forwarded a sext or have had a sext of theirs forwarded without the consent of all parties. This is behavior that has led to arrests for child pornography in cases across North America.

In my practice, I have seen adolescents who have had their own private images shared without their consent, and I've also seen kids get into legal trouble for distributing such content, and this has led me to believe that sexting is like a gateway drug. Kids who engage in it, whether they initiated the texts or not, become desensitized to sexualized images and actions, more easily progress to performing oral sex, and then move more quickly toward having intercourse than those who don't.

Simply being aware that this risk exists, and that such a progression is happening among teens and even some tweens, is an important first step for parents. You must take decisive action the first time your child engages in any sexualized activity on social media. This activity could be simply posting a provocative selfie or asking another person to send a similar picture; or it could involve a sexual chat with a person he may or may not know in real life; or maybe it's making an explicit comment on someone else's post or sharing images of others without their consent. Each of these is an example of a situation in which parents should intervene and talk with their child about the seriousness of this behavior. This book will help you know what to look for and how to handle the situation.

Communication Is Key

Parents can prevent or mitigate the flood of sexualized material facing their kids through the simplest of acts: communication.

At its best, sex is an expression of love and intimacy between two people who are deeply connected. When experienced this way, sex is part of a healthy relationship that can last for a long time. Even when the relationship is not a lasting one, deep feelings and honorable actions can set the stage for a solid relationship when the right person does come along.

At its worst, sex is a commodity exchanged for popularity or acceptance. When used this way, or when it happens too early (during the preteen or early teen years), sex can be soul destroying. Because early experiences set the stage for later relationships, they need to be taken seriously. Talk to your preteen about both the psychological and physical ramifications of sex. Being educated on the facts around safer sex can help to keep the body safe but does not necessarily protect the psyche—the mind, soul, and spirit.

Most adolescents understand the basic physical mechanics of sex. What you can help your child learn before puberty even starts is how to evaluate

SEVEN POINT Parental Compass

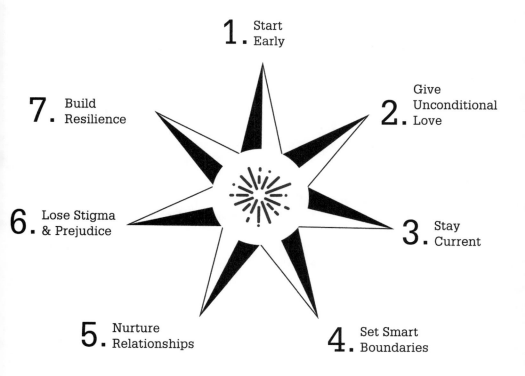

1. Start Early
2. Give Unconditional Love
3. Stay Current
4. Set Smart Boundaries
5. Nurture Relationships
6. Lose Stigma & Prejudice
7. Build Resilience

content he sees, unpack things he hears, and then make healthy judgments about how to behave. When the conversation about bodies starts before changes begin, your child will come to you first for advice, help, and wisdom as he moves into his teenage years.

Hopefully, this is the impetus that you, as a parent, need to overcome any sense that sex is a taboo subject or any embarrassment you may feel. You may not have felt comfortable talking about sex with your parents, but your child needs to be able to talk to you about it. It's one of the most effective ways you can help keep your kids safe.

Unfortunately, too few parents talk with their children about sex and sexual issues. In 2015, the *Journal of Children and Media* reported that, although boys are more likely to look at pornography, parents were no more likely to talk to them about pornography than they were to girls. Results also showed that when a child was caught viewing pornography, the rate of parental involvement and dialogue rose after the incident. Parents are being reactive instead of proactive, and this has to change!

Talk with your children, directly and unequivocally, about their sexuality and about what they may see on the Internet and social media. And not just once. You need to continue to have conversations, react to situations that come up, and remind kids about healthy choices and your expectations for their good behavior.

My goal is to help parents and children build rapport, trust, and connection. The more your child understands that she can turn to you for answers and share questions without shame, the stronger your bond will be. That bond will be your most valuable tool moving forward. The aim is to raise strong, self-assured children who are ready to deal with anything that comes at them.

Good communication works! Research—and my own clinical experience—shows that adolescents who have repeated, open, casual communication about sex, sexuality, and development with their parents are more likely to have a closer relationship with them. Lecturing by parents, on the other hand, can have an effect opposite to what parents intend. A 2015 study in the *Journal of Adolescent Health* found that the quality of parents' communication with their teens about dating and sex predicted sexual behavior. In particular, the study found that lecturing was associated with a higher likelihood that teens would have sexual intercourse.

That's not all. In a 2017 study published in *Sexuality Research & Social Policy*, many young adults said they appreciated that their parents talked often about sex, and many wished their parents had talked more about sex. They also wanted their parents to be *more* open and honest when discussing sex, dating, and other issues such as sexual orientation, and they specifically wanted their parents to be open to questions.

When I began to see in my clinical practice climbing numbers of children struggling to deal with our hypersexualized world, I realized how fast the landscape was shifting. Families are dealing with complex issues, many arising from kids being exposed to sexual content before they are prepared to handle it. When I'm presented with a big problem, and family members in a session are feeling overwhelmed, I go back to the basics of my training as a therapist. I look at the research and literature that's been done and synthesize it into a tool that's appropriate for the situation. My Parental Compass emerged out of that process, and it's meant as a guide for parents who are about to sail into the waters of the preteen and teen years, as well as for those who are already navigating choppy seas and need to find a way through the storm. I have used this tool in my practice for years, and it has helped hundreds of families along their journey. I know it will help you in yours.

What Is the Parental Compass?

Simply put, the Parental Compass is a framework of seven guiding principles that parents can use to ensure their children know that they are valued for who they are and that they have an ally in their parents. It's a tool you can use to help stay focused on true north throughout your parenting journey.

I developed the Parental Compass after a series of clinical sessions with families who were all facing issues with their young children brought on by heightened sexual exposure. Coming out of those sessions, again and again, I felt frustrated and concerned that the tools and techniques available to clinicians like me were inadequate for helping families in the midst of crisis. So I worked to formulate a flexible plan that could help parents guide their children. As I organized my thoughts, I went through the body of literature, researching current issues and trends. Then I reflected on what I'd learned as it related to the experiences I was seeing in my practices. I assembled the key points to create a tool that would be easy for families to use and would offer practical, actionable direction for getting to their ultimate objective: building resilience. The Parental Compass was born.

Each of the seven points stands on its own as a best parenting practice. However, each point also works collectively with the others to provide a framework that will help your child make it through any challenge she may face in life. So these particular practices will help you protect your children from the dangers of our hypersexualized landscape and also mitigate the effects if kids do wander into trouble. Guided by these principles, you'll be able to tackle any issues as a family and help your child come out the other side stronger, wiser, and more resilient than ever.

Confronting Complex Challenges

This fast-moving world of ours is creating increasingly complex and unexpected challenges for families. If there ever was a parenting "rule book," highly charged topics ranging from sexting to sexualized bullying to online pornography have rendered it obsolete. So I wanted to look beyond old rules and consider values as a framework for guiding parents.

The Parental Compass has two key goals:

- To strengthen the parent-child bond

- To support parents in becoming effective problem solvers

Forging a strong parent-child bond isn't without challenges. Kids will be kids, and they will test your limits and push your buttons because that's what they do best. You may tear your hair out dealing with them sometimes, yet if you've built a strong bond, it will endure. A child may feel like he is grounded more often than he's allowed out, and that you're the most unfair parent in the world, but kids do best in highly structured relationships that are also warm and loving. In such relationships, limits exist and are consistently and fairly enforced.

Though enforcing limits can cause friction and may stretch the parent-child bond at times, that bond won't break. It will actually become stronger in the end. A home that is high in warmth and structure allows a child to develop a consistent and regulated perspective on the world. Additionally, a good parent-child relationship helps a child form problem-solving skills. So short-term frustration may ensue when you enforce boundaries, but the long-term benefits far outweigh the momentary setbacks.

The values-based guidance embedded in my Parental Compass also helps you lay a foundation from which to problem solve. There is an acronym I use, borrowed from military strategists, to describe our changing world to parents who are wondering what got them there: VUCA. Ours world can seem full of volatility, uncertainty, complexity, and ambiguity. Because of the fast pace of change, any set of rigid parenting rules, including those your own parents may have used, quickly becomes outdated. Parents need to prepare for the unexpected, for things they never lived through themselves. The Compass steers your decisions but offers flexibility in determining the solution that best fits your family and the situation at hand.

I designed the Parental Compass to be easy to remember and to use. It represents twenty years of psychological knowledge synthesized into a single, all-encompassing tool. Although it can't answer every parenting question you'll ever face (no such tool exists, as there is often no single clear answer), it gives you a framework for dealing with the challenges that come at you and your family.

Hitting the Reset Button

I chose a circular tool—a compass—on purpose. Growing up is not a strictly linear progress with a clearly defined end point, and parents and children will need to travel around that circle many times as children grow. All the points on the Parental Compass work in tandem, and no one point is effective without support from the others.

You may be reading through these Compass points and worrying that it's too late, that your relationship with your child is already off-base or that the situation is too far gone. Please know that it's *never* too late! You can work toward a strong parent-child relationship even if your kids are in their late teens, and problem solving in a healthy way is a skill that will serve you, and your kids, for a lifetime. The values are timeless. If things haven't been going well, you can press the reset button with your child.

Take a deep breath and then say to your child, "I don't think this conversation is going the way we want it to

go. Our relationship is what is most important. So, what can we do to start over?" Then talk about what it is that you want to do differently:

- Bring up ways you and your child can better communicate and understand each other.

- Consider whether spending more time together needs to be a priority.

- Solicit your child's point of view and ask what changes she would like to see.

- Follow through on all commitments made during a reset.

I have seen in my practice that kids are responsive to this technique. A reset relieves what can seem like a pressure-cooker environment to a child, especially one who feels like she is in a lose-lose situation. Kids really like being able to share their own thoughts, and talking openly with your child is a good practice to put in place before she hits the teen years. Keep in mind that this reset will only *truly* work if you walk the talk and follow through on the commitments you make.

Moving Forward Together

You have years ahead with your children, and what you can do *right now* is start to set things right for the future. Parents often come into my office and say they wished they had come in years earlier. They feel helpless and that there's no possible solution for their problems. When they get to this point, they may blame themselves, feeling like they let a problem with their children go on too long and now a fix is out of sight.

If you or someone you know is in this situation, please know there is always hope. You have a chance to repair the relationship. What will it take? Lots of hard work and some purposeful conversations and thoughtful decisions. You can start by having a family meeting. Sit down, gather everyone's input, avoid the blame game, and then make a plan for moving forward together.

When it comes to situations involving sexuality, the conversations can be awkward at first, but they are crucial for your family's well-being. Broaching the subject is often the hardest part, so I encourage you to take a deep breath and just dive in. (Think about it: It's easier to dive into a calm pool than a roiling ocean, so having the conversations *before* a problem crops up is to everyone's benefit!) Once you've started the conversation, the awkwardness melts away—even the most apprehensive parents confirm this. The more you talk about sex and other potentially awkward topics, the easier it gets.

When you make the decision to improve your relationship with your children, how can you hold yourself accountable? First, be self-aware and observant of your own behaviors, as well as reflective about how you achieved your goals. Metacognition—thinking about thinking—is also helpful, and journaling can strengthen this high-level process. Reflect on a negative event or a mistake you made on a particular day: How did you feel? What did you think? How did you react? Did your actions accomplish what you wanted? What do you wish you had done differently? Recording these events will help you catch yourself before you react poorly, as you'll be more attuned and aware of the triggers. In this way, journaling is a powerful technique that can help you change your behavior and your reactions over time.

***

I framed the best of what I know into my Parental Compass to reinforce the idea that sometimes there are no clear answers and we need to make our way through foggy emotional weather. We will likely need to guide our children through experiences that we've never lived through ourselves. The Compass allows us to apply the best of current parenting principles so we can navigate these challenges. The next seven chapters will take the points one at a time, expanding each one so you can see how to execute it and how it dovetails with the other principles. Up first, start talking with your children about sex and sexual issues early—most likely earlier than you imagined.

In each chapter, I provide questions to get you thinking about your family in relation to the material I cover. Please take a moment to write your responses in the space provided. My intention is for you to find these responses helpful as you integrate the principles of the compass into your life.

How does the current sexual landscape make you feel? What are your goals for helping your child navigate it?

_____

_____

_____

_____

_____

_____

_____

_____

_____

_____

_____

_____

_____

_____

_____

_____

_____

_____

_____

_____

_____

_____

2

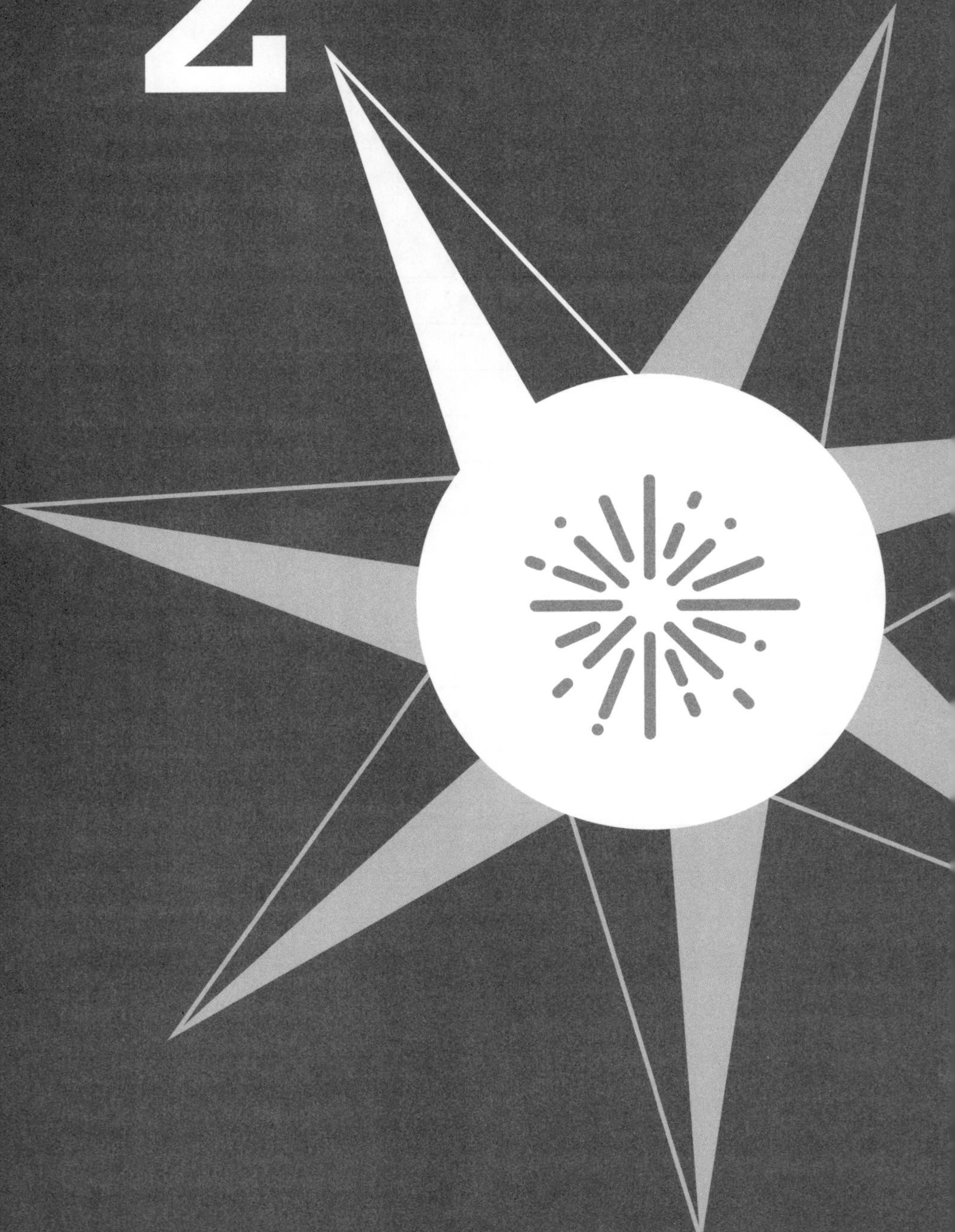

CHAPTER 2

START EARLY

From their toddler years—when children begin to gain understanding that the self is distinct from others—our children need to learn that everyone has a personal space around them that others should not enter unless the person allows it. With toddlers, I use the term "personal bubble" to explain the concept. During those early years, potty training is a natural way to begin sharing these lessons. Use correct names for body parts and answer questions in age-appropriate ways. Following are some examples of questions a young child might ask, together with answers using accurate terms and conveying age-appropriate information:

Child: *Is there a baby in that lady's tummy?*
Parent: Babies grow inside a woman's uterus, near her stomach. It's a special place that is just for babies to grow in.

Child: *Where do babies come from?*
Parent: A baby is made with an egg and a sperm. Eggs come from a woman's body and sperm come from a man's body. The baby grows inside a woman's body until it is ready to be born.

Child: *How come boys stand up to pee, but girls sit down?*
Parent: Everyone has a urethra, which is where pee comes out. A boy's is inside his penis, and a girl's is inside her vulva. That is why boys can stand up.

Child: *Why do I have to wear pants/underwear/a bathing suit?*
Parent: We wear clothes to protect our genitals from germs, and also so that nobody else can see or touch them—because they are private parts of our bodies.

As a child gets older, these conversations can—indeed, should—grow up with them. Kids' normal behavior will offer many natural opportunities to begin these kinds of conversations; keeping their hands to themselves on the playground, maintaining privacy between siblings, and handling disputes properly are a few of the situations that can spark discussion.

Whenever a child has a question about his body, where babies come from, or something he saw on a video or heard from a friend, parents need to answer in honest, accurate, and direct ways. If you wonder what's appropriate for your child's age, know that it's better to err on the side of giving more information than less, as kids these days are exposed to a lot of information from outside the home. Having ongoing conversations sets parents up as go-to people for kids when they have questions. That's crucial for your children's tween/teen years. If they feel safe talking with you now, they'll be more apt to come to you when a more serious situation develops.

FamilySparks has a picture book for toddlers titled *Where Do Babies Come From?,* written specifically to help parents start conversations about sex when their children are very young. If you're starting that early, you're ahead of the game. Because children open up more easily when they are younger, the habit of talking about bodies, behavior, and sexuality will have time to form and stick. Even if you didn't begin in toddlerhood, it's never too late to make sure a child knows he is in charge of his own body.

Unfortunately, tweens often find themselves in confusing situations, even if you started talking with them about their bodies when they were still in the womb! For most, the years before and during puberty will be riddled with awkwardness, mood swings, fluctuating feelings, and uncomfortable situations. The message that your child is in charge of his own body is incredibly important. From learning good hygiene to knowing what physical changes to expect to navigating fledgling relationships, young people ten to eighteen years of age need to know, understand, and respect their own bodies. When our kids have an understanding of tough topics, they can make responsible choices rather than going into tricky social or sexual situations blind.

As we saw in chapter 1, the danger of a child encountering inappropriate content online is now sky high. Sexual images or videos depicting sex acts are so pervasive online today that it is becoming rare for a tween *not* to see this type of content. So they must be prepared. A child who knows that he might come across explicit material can process it and make a better decision about what to do than a child who has no idea what he is seeing or why.

How to Start Conversations About Sex

I cannot stress enough the importance of having comprehensive and age-appropriate conversations with your children about sex and sexual issues. You wouldn't send them to a friend's house or on an errand alone without making sure they knew where they were going, what to be careful of along the way, and what to do if they hit a roadblock, right? You'd make sure they understand the directions, why one intersection is more dangerous than another, and how to call you for help if needed.

The same principles apply to conversations about sex. Your child's health and well-being are increasingly tied to making sure she can navigate these unfamiliar roads successfully. So let her know the facts about sex, in clear and straightforward terms. You'll want to make sure she understands that some of her friends may talk about sex differently, but that your family's values are set for a reason. Be sure that she knows to come to you if she sees something confusing, if a friend says something she doesn't understand, or if someone behaves in a way that makes her uncomfortable.

Accuracy counts heavily here. You must be forthright, so your child understands exactly what you are saying about sex and sexual issues. Like getting a vaccine, learning the facts about sex inoculates your children against the effects of disturbing sexual content online or via friends. If she is prepared for what's coming, she can either avoid the pitfalls altogether or, at the very least, not feel caught off guard when confronted by graphic content that might trouble a child who is less prepared.

There are two key types of conversations that you can use to introduce the topic of sex:

1. Icebreaker conversations

2. Milestone conversations

ICEBREAKER CONVERSATIONS

A chat about one thing can often lead to a discussion of something else entirely. If you have a plan to segue a conversation in a certain direction, your digression can seem off the cuff and less like a lecture or a rehearsed speech. This tactic allows your message to sink in without triggering the usual defense mechanisms a tween or teen may put up.

Ease in to the conversation by asking questions about your child's day, just as you may typically do:

- "Who did you connect with today?"

- "Did you have an aha moment this week?"

- "What's something you've never told me before?"

- "Tell me something that's going on in your world that you don't think I know about."

Parents who ask kids questions need to really listen to the answers. Follow up on any tidbits of information they share. You'll want to tailor your continued conversation to your child's specific responses, but here are some general ideas for following up on each of my proposed icebreakers:

- "That's nice that you met a new friend. If you want to invite your friend to come over this weekend, let me know."

- "Ooh, that's a pretty big aha. How is that going to change how you do things from now on?"

- "I'm glad you told me that, it's important for me to know what's going on with you so I can help when you have questions."

- "Well, you might think I don't know anything about that. Maybe you'll be surprised when I tell you that I did know and was just giving you some space to think about it."

Each of these responses may lead to a larger conversation. Keeping the lines of communication open between yourself and your child sets the stage for good communication throughout her adolescence. Of course, if your child tires of sharing the details of her life, as tweens and teens sometimes do, save your questions and bring them up at another time. Following up later could also be a good way to bring your spouse or another family member into the conversation.

- "The other day you mentioned a friend's name I hadn't heard before. How did you meet Ryan?"

- "You know, you had that aha moment last week. Are you keeping it in mind as you focus on what's coming up?"

- "I thought a little more about what you said yesterday and wanted you to know something else . . . "

- "Remember when you said you didn't think I knew anything about (insert topic)? I was talking with (spouse) about it, and s/he wanted to talk with you about it too."

Another way to set the stage for open discussion is to start casual conversations about relationships. Yes, it can get awkward. That's part of talking about tricky subjects, and the sooner you accept that it's going to be a little awkward, the sooner you can push past it.

The car is a great place to have these conversations because you're both looking forward rather than at each other, making the moment less intense. You're also trapped together for a little while, so there are fewer distractions than there might be in another setting. You can start a conversation with a story about yourself. For example:

- "You know, I'm not sure you've ever heard the *real* story about how I fell in love with your mom/dad . . . "

- "I was thinking today about my first crush, and that I was about your age when it happened . . . "

- "Last night, Grandpa said he ran into one of my old flames from back home, and it got me thinking about the time when . . . "

- "That song always reminds me of one of my good friends because . . . "

Sharing stories like these can bring you and your child closer together. It is also a way to model the kinds of decisions about relationships and love that you want to encourage without sounding like you are lecturing. One word of caution: Make sure you're sharing a story to be helpful. If you're estranged from your child's other parent, don't use this time to try to sway your child to your side of a dispute. If you have any past trauma in your life, try not to burden your child with details beyond her age level and understanding. If it's a story you feel is important to share, focus on how you made it through your challenges and the decisions you made that were good choices. During an icebreaker conversation, the positive side of a story is usually the most effective foundation on which to build a closer relationship.

MILESTONE CONVERSATIONS

When a milestone age or event comes up, you can use it as a way to open up a dialogue with your child about sexuality. Most likely, she'll have questions around these time periods anyway, so your conversation can flow naturally from your child's prompts.

Occasions like shopping for a bra, buying that first razor, or selecting an outfit for the first school dance are milestones that can be treated like a mini celebration. This way, you become an active participant in your child's growing up within the context of talking and shopping. Because body image—for both girls and boys—can be a huge issue, often amplified by harmful messages in mass culture and on social media, parents need to underscore healthy attitudes and savvy consumerism.

- When shopping, you could say, for example: "You know, when you see pictures of models advertising different kinds of underwear, that isn't the way regular people look, right? The editors Photoshop all those pictures to look a certain way, so don't ever compare yourself with what you see because you're real and those photos aren't."

- With your daughter's first period, you have a chance to ask: "Do you understand why this is happening, and what it means about your body?"

- As your son approaches puberty, you could use an upcoming birthday as the impetus for conversation: "Do you understand what changes are going to happen to your body soon? It's different from the changes happening to girls. If you have any questions about that, you can ask me."

- When you're shopping for that perfect dress or new suit, you could ask: "Do your friends ever talk about kissing at the school dance, or even having sex? A lot of my friends talked about that, and I was confused at first because I didn't understand what they meant. I want you to know that you can always come to me to find out, and I promise I'll tell you the truth and I won't be embarrassed."

- Anytime you're talking about sexual issues and your child seems to be embarrassed, or admits that he is, address it head on: "You might feel embarrassed about the changes going on in your body, but it's not embarrassing to me. Dad [or Mom] and I have already been through it, so you can always talk to us."

Some parents find it useful to read books or watch videos about difficult subjects with their children. A list of resources at the back of this book offers some suggestions for talking with your child or preteen about sexuality, body safety, relationships, and more.

When having conversations with your kids, keep the following points in mind:

- Always tell kids the truth, even if the question is an awkward one.

- Use the correct names for body parts. Young people are better able to maintain their boundaries when they understand the proper terminology.

- When your child asks a question, always reply with an appreciation that she came to you: "That's a good question!" or "I'm glad you asked me about that." This sets you up to be the person your child trusts with hard questions, no matter how uncomfortable.

- Respond in as straightforward and accurate a manner as possible, even if the question shocks you. There will be time later to figure out from where the question originated.

- If a complete answer to the question would be inappropriate for your child's age, tell him you need time to think about how to explain it. This will buy you a little time to formulate an appropriate answer.

Start Early with Technology Rules

You now know how easy it is for kids to stumble on the plethora of easily accessible sexual information online. Even a simple online search can direct kids to highly inappropriate material, and sometimes parental controls don't help. Pornographic sites may purposely use children's toys or other innocuous objects to lure hits, and a search for those keywords can unwittingly lead to the site. A curious child could continue to explore the linked images or not know how to get out of the site once it comes up on the device. Once the child clicks, a search engine's algorithms can show more of the same content.

This easy access to pornography and other explicit content is the reason you need to start "The Other Talk" when kids are young—this is the talk about the kinds of inappropriate content kids may encounter online, how to handle it, and how to avoid it.

Although your child may not be among those who are exposed early, you need to know that the possibility exists. Stay apprised of trends and issues related to cybersafety (we'll talk more about this in chapter 4, "Stay Current"), and from time to time put your child's favorite toy or sports hero into a search engine to see what pops up. Sit alongside younger children when they go online to show them how to search and interact safely, and use parental controls and monitor older children's use.

There's no need to be sneaky about monitoring your children online. As a parent, you must make sure that the granting of device privileges comes with expectations that your children will behave appropriately online—and you need to spell out, with specifics, what appropriate behavior means. Before giving your child his own device, establish an online safety plan. The following plan, developed by FamilySparks, sets limits that encourage healthy online behavior. Adapt the rules as needed for your own family:

1. Only post status updates/photos if you have permission from the others involved.

2. Only post things that will make people smile.

3. Only "like" or "share" positive content—not gossip, rumors, or mean comments.

4. Only post things you would be comfortable with everybody seeing. (Examples include grandparents, teachers, strangers, and so on. You never know who will see your post, even if you think your settings are private.)

5. Always ask before putting any words or phrases into an Internet search engine. Parents can help ensure that spelling is correct and results are appropriate.

6. Never click links, pop-ups, ads, or offers without showing them to parents first.

Creating a plan for use of social media and online tools is a crucial part of the "Start Early" point on the Parental Compass. You need to roll out your expectations before your child has a dedicated device, if possible, and you must continue to enforce those expectations as your child matures. Emphasizing Internet safety when kids are young goes hand in hand with talking about their bodies and respecting personal space from a very early age.

The child who learns at age two what happens when she goes pee is the child who understands at four that no one is allowed to touch her body without permission; this is the child who at six uses her words rather than her fists to solve problems in school; it is the child who, at eight, stands up for a classmate who is picked on for being different; and it is the ten-year-old who tells her parents when she sees an inappropriate video online. This early foundation is the bedrock upon which your child bases decisions for the rest of her life.

Encountering Pornography

Sometimes outside events shape the way we understand the world and how we begin to make sense of sexuality. Stumbling upon pornography can affect children's foundational understanding of sexuality. Pornography is designed to entertain, excite, and push limits. It often involves a power dynamic in which a man is able to do whatever he wants to a woman, perhaps without consent and with little to no consideration for her pleasure. The scenes depicted are not accurate representations of what happens in a healthy sexual relationship and should not be held up as an example of love.

Young people who have been exposed to pornographic content may think that's what sex is supposed to be like, but it's not. People should not feel uncomfortable about having sex; if you are uncomfortable about something, you should not do it.

Our young men need to realize that, in real life, acting out some of the things depicted in pornography can lead to charges of sexual assault and rape. Our young women need to understand that they have the right to feel comfortable and safe in their sexual encounters, and that no partner should expect them to go along with sex acts they're uncomfortable with just because those acts appear in pornography. Healthy beliefs begin when our boys and girls are taught ownership of their bodies, honest communication, and ways to handle confusing situations in their early years.

Sonia's Story

In my practice, I sometimes see clients on an emergency basis. One such case began with a frantic call from a single dad named William. The story he told me on the phone was chilling.

William's daughter, Sonia, who had just turned ten, was working on a science project for school. He had given her a computer for her birthday, and she was in her room alone working on her project. The topic was bacteria, and Internet research was required.

A little backstory will help you understand the situation better. Sonia's mom passed away from cancer before she turned two, so it's always been just Sonia and William. Too young to really remember her mother, Sonia only knows life with a single dad.

William has done great raising her on his own, as neither set of grandparents lives nearby.

At the point of the emergency phone call, William hadn't yet had "The Talk" with his daughter. That's a milestone he was hoping to put off for another year. Sonia's school doesn't broach the subject of sex until fifth grade, so William thought he had plenty of time. The longer he could keep his little girl innocent of the ways of the world, the better, in his mind.

But on this day, he walked into his daughter's bedroom to check on her before dinner and found a disturbing scene: Sonia was on her bed, naked, with her legs and one arm duct-taped to the bedposts. She was crying because she couldn't get free.

At first, William thought someone was in their home abusing his daughter. He yelled, "Who did this to you?" and then grabbed Sonia's softball bat and frantically ran through the house searching for an intruder. Sonia was now crying so hard she couldn't make him understand. It was a long while before he could truly comprehend what had happened.

Within a couple of minutes, William realized there was no one in the house and came back to Sonia, removing the tape from her arm and legs. She calmed down after a few minutes but she really didn't know how to explain what happened. He

kept asking questions and then went to the computer and uncovered the truth: As she searched online for her science project, Sonia misspelled "organism" as "orgasm" and stumbled onto a hardcore pornographic site.

William and I had a phone conversation that evening, and father and daughter came to my office a couple of days later. I was able to determine, and to explain to William, that what Sonia was doing with the duct tape was reenacting the bondage scene she'd witnessed online. While a child simulating bondage is very disturbing, reenacting a traumatic experience is a common way for children to try to process something they've seen.

A FOUNDATIONAL EVENT

Children cannot make sense of what they see when they view pornography, and those images bounce around in their psyches. A child who's witnessed something traumatic reengages in the event over and over, trying to figure it out. This is often done via play. Children who are car crash victims often re-create what happened to them with toy cars, just as children who witness gun violence may pretend to shoot others in play. Their brains are trying to make sense of what they've seen so, just as adults run through a tragedy in their heads over and over again, children may reenact scenarios. The replaying of the event can also occur in nightmares and flashbacks.

Because hardcore pornography was Sonia's very first exposure to sex, and she had no foundation for healthy sexual behavior, the video she saw became part of her foundation, one that would take a great deal of work to mitigate. Luckily for Sonia, William made it a priority to get her to a psychologist's office for help and continued to support healing in the months to come.

The first order of business in counselling was to ensure that Sonia did not believe in any way that it was her fault she had seen the pornographic images. This is crucial because it is very common for children to think they did something wrong, and they can internalize that self-blame. Although they may not ever talk about those feelings, keeping them buried deep within can cause other issues down the road, so recognizing she was not to blame was an important first step for Sonia.

Next I helped Sonia emotionally process what she saw. This work occurred over a number of sessions, often with William present. We discussed what was inappropriate about the images she saw. We also began to discuss sexuality in healthy terms. I encouraged Sonia to ask as many questions as she had, and I supported her father in responding in an honest and straightforward manner. I also encouraged William to listen carefully to what Sonia was asking and to respond only to her questions—not

to add or elaborate on things that she did not really want to know yet. I call this "just-enough responding." These question-and-answer periods in our counseling sessions set up a safe space for both father and daughter to truly open up to each other and also gave them a way to ease into a comfort zone of discussing issues of sexuality. I was helping them build the foundation they should have already had.

RAMIFICATIONS

Even with immediate help, Sonia's experience couldn't be erased from her psyche and it rippled outward to affect other areas of her life. She made some comments to kids at school about what she'd seen, again as a way to make sense of the experience. As you can imagine, this was concerning to other parents. Without understanding the situation, which they were not privy to, those parents didn't want their children to play with Sonia because they felt her behavior was aberrant. (There was even an email chain among some of the moms at school detailing how she was a "bad influence.") As a result, Sonia ended up ostracized at school and in the neighborhood, which led to her being bullied.

Would something else have caused the bullying anyway? Perhaps. Bullying is quite pervasive among kids today. Sonia's experience and the psychological trauma she suffered may not have been linked directly with the bullying she faced, however, anytime a child's name or behavior is associated with sex, or even sexually tinged behavior, she or he becomes a target for either ridicule or emulation. In a vicious cycle, Sonia lashed out at the mean kids at school, hitting one boy on the playground when she'd gotten fed up with his teasing. Because she was the one who resorted to physical violence, she was perceived as an aggressor and suspended. All of this reinforced the negative view she had come to have of herself in the world.

During the initial years of a child's life, usually until about age twelve, she develops important beliefs about herself in the world, a sort of mental framework that helps her interpret incoming information. In psychology, we call this "schema formation." The impact of childhood trauma can be much greater than trauma sustained in adulthood because early trauma affects the process of schema formation.

Here is another way of thinking about this: In these early years, a child is being wired for how to behave in the world. A traumatic experience can act like a computer virus that negatively affects the operating system. Consequently, the child can start to believe, inaccurately, that there is something wrong with her deep inside that cannot be fixed. She can also start thinking of the world as dangerous and unpredictable. These underlying beliefs can affect her choices and

behaviors for years to come, thereby negatively affecting her social interactions, academic success, and entire life path.

William didn't realize how easily accessible sexual information is online. Sadly, parents today must expect that their child will find online pornography and should think through their response in advance so they can react in an appropriate manner. Here are some ways to respond if your child tells you about sexual content she found online, or if you learn in another way that she accessed such material, perhaps by noting it in the computer's search history:

- "I'm really glad you told me about this. How are you feeling about what you saw?"

- "I bet that was very confusing/scary/weird for you. Thank you for telling me. Do you have any questions about anything you saw?"

- "You are not in trouble, but we do need to talk about this. Pornography was made for adults, and it's not an example of how people should act in real life. It's also not appropriate for kids to watch. Will you please tell me how you found this/who showed this to you?"

- "I understand that this has made you feel uncomfortable. I would feel uncomfortable too. Let's make a plan together so that you don't stumble across something like this again."

If William had started talking with Sonia about sex and sexual content earlier, her reaction to what she saw may not have been so extreme. Though the content would still have been shocking, the harm she suffered would likely not have been as severe. It's important to note that there is no magic button that would have prevented the situation altogether, but early and sustained conversations about body parts, body image, and sex may have laid a foundation that would have sent Sonia directly to her father when she encountered the hardcore pornography. William would have been able to explain what she saw in words she could understand, and her mind wouldn't have kept the images bouncing around in her psyche for as long. She likely would not have reenacted the scene, which traumatized her all over again.

Although William could have done a great deal more on the first Compass point, Start Early, he excelled in many others and was able to help Sonia recover from the trauma. He was able to build up her resilience over the years, and that played a huge role in her recovery. You'll read more about resilience and how you can build it in your own children in chapter 8.

William's handling of his daughter's trauma stemmed from his unconditional love for her. Healing took some time, but his meaningful support of Sonia's psychological and emotional needs made all the difference for her. He put her needs first and made sure to protect her from feelings of shame.

***

Behind all your conversations about important issues such as sex is the idea that you are building a foundation of love, trust, and openness that will last throughout your kids' adolescent years. You may not feel this at times, but you are the most important person in your child's life, and your unconditional love holds a great deal of power. While loving our children might seem like the kind of thing that we parents do naturally, unconditional love can be demonstrated in a mindful, thoughtful way that offers crucial psychological benefits. We'll look at these valuable advantages in the next chapter.

Tell me something that's going on in your world that you think I don't know.

Riley in my class is going out with Gavin.

Oh, I didn't know that people were starting to see each other in your grade. What do you think of that?

Hmm...

It's kind of exciting but also, it feels weird.

I understand what you're saying. It feels less weird when you're older. Different kids will feel ready for this at different times. When the time is right for you, it won't feel so weird.

Okay, that's good to know!

Who had these early conversations with you? How were they handled?
What will you do the same and what will you do differently?

_____

_____

_____

_____

_____

_____

_____

_____

_____

_____

_____

_____

_____

_____

_____

_____

_____

_____

_____

_____

_____

_____

_____

_____

_____

When will you start (or continue) the conversation with your child?
What will you say to them? Be specific and do your best to follow
through.

CHAPTER 3

GIVE UNCONDITIONAL LOVE

While you're raising your children, you may not feel as though your input carries much weight, but the truth is that parents are the number-one influencers in a child's life. That is one thing that has not changed in parenting. However, that position of influence is something you need to cultivate. You want to advance yourself as *the* go-to person for your child.

The unconditional love of a parent for a child is the biggest kind of love, and should dictate all your parenting decisions. Your love is the deepest form of validation for your child, and it provides a solid foundation from which he can ask life's big questions. It allows you to put your child first, and is the driving force that nurtures your child and offers protection. This type of love makes sure your child is heard and understood, especially when he has made a mistake.

Mistakes often stem from curiosity, so your child's missteps make great learning opportunities. When a child can learn from a mistake, we say he is developing a growth mindset, which helps set him up to reframe mistakes

as life lessons over the course of his development. A child (or adult!) with a growth mindset doesn't let a mistake throw him off track permanently and accepts that most things in life have a learning curve. Kids who are afraid to make mistakes won't put themselves out there.

When your child makes a mistake:

- Reframe the mistake as a learning opportunity, which promotes a growth mindset.

- Never give your child the silent treatment.

- Never use shame or guilt-inducing strategies as discipline.

Parents' relationships with their children are always works in progress, but unconditional love is a constant. This chapter not only walks you through the reasons your unconditional love is so important to your child, it explains how to be intentional in conveying that love.

A parent's unconditional love creates a strong bond between parent and child, which bolsters the child's mental well-being. This doesn't mean you must have a perfect relationship with your child—we all know the tween and teen years can be . . . challenging. Discipline is still necessary. But the unconditional love you offer forms a solid relationship foundation and encourages your child to ask questions and share concerns about difficult topics without fear of being judged or scolded. Knowing that your love is absolute can also help your child feel less fearful and more able to bounce back from problems.

Building a Foundation

When a parent and a child have built a solid foundation for their relationship, the benefits are multiplied by a thousand. Your relationship is the cornerstone of your child's psyche. It gives him a steady foundation for his future development, allowing him to build resilience (which I'll talk about more in chapter 8). Our fast-paced world may change around your children, but you, as their parent, will always remain their rock.

Parents can model healthy, loving relationships with each other while fostering emotional intimacy with all family members. Of course, you tell your family you love them every chance you get. I hope you also tell them that you like them and what, specifically, you like about them.

There are many ways to do this, and your family probably has some great ways you've established bonds over the years. Make sure your partner, kids, and anyone else in your household knows how happy they make you, and that they are your whole life. Express your emotions. Put notes in their lunch boxes when your kids are in elementary school. Text your teens. In the following sections, you'll find some additional ideas for conveying your love and techniques to make the conversations flow more smoothly.

BOOKENDS

Bookend your child's day: Make sure to have a meaningful connection in the morning and before bed, despite the many activities that may occur throughout the day. One great way to build this bookend relationship is to eat meals together as a family. This is a simple but powerful way to strengthen bonds with your family.

Even though it's hard to schedule regular mealtimes into our busy lives, I recommend families do so as often as possible. It's never too late to start. If you haven't been able to do this much in the past, know that every meal together counts: breakfast, lunch, or dinner. Keep your meals technology free, as much as you can. Many families keep a basket in their kitchen and have everyone place their devices in it during the meal. As technology is increasingly integrated into the items we use and expectations for rapid replies to messages go up, disconnecting becomes harder, but do your best to find a way.

Mealtimes are the best time to talk about your day, ask questions, and learn details. This is true whether it's a stand-up breakfast as everyone gets ready in the morning, a homemade three-course dinner, or fast food from the drive-through on the way to soccer practice. Make as much of mealtimes as possible.

TRADITION!

Creating and observing family traditions are other ways for parents and children to build a strong foundation. From preparing holiday foods to giving funny birthday cards to commemorating milestones, special moments help give a family its unique character. Even young children can sense when something is a tradition, and they rely on these rituals as the threads that weave their childhood together.

Some families have circumstances or interruptions that make certain traditions tough to uphold, such as divorce, death, or illness in the family; blended families from varying religious backgrounds (e.g., some members celebrate Christmas while others celebrate Hanukkah); or living apart from extended family who host holiday celebrations. If that's the case, I encourage you to create new traditions for your family. If your child is

old enough, ask him to help you come up with some of those traditions. In this way, you'll continue to build that solid foundation for a relationship with your child.

THE 5:1 CONCEPT

Focusing on the positive will go a long way with your child. Criticism is easier for children to hear and accept from a parent when it comes with a lot of cushioning. If we are too critical of our kids without balancing it with a lot of positive reinforcement, we can end up pushing them away. Many children simply shut down in the face of criticism.

We don't want them to shut down, we want them to open up, so I talk with parents about using the 5:1 concept with their kids. It's simple! You want to say five kind words for every critique or correction. This ensures that the positive outweighs the negative. Sharing thoughts that are encouraging, that validate his feelings, and that affirm her happiness as important to you will reap many benefits.

The 5:1 concept ensures that you can find the positive in your kids—that you actually look for it every chance you get—so share with them your pride, your happiness, and your belief in them. There will always be things that they can do better, but by making sure you highlight their good words and deeds you encourage more of that behavior.

THE HAMBURGER STRATEGY

The Hamburger Strategy is a way to bundle advice for your child—the "meat" of the matter—inside two pieces of "bread." Thus, the stuff in the middle—the criticisms/corrections—will be masked by the deliciousness of the bread, the positive words.

"Hamburger" formula =
positive comment +
area needing improvement +
positive comment

If you use the Hamburger Strategy, you'll never provide too many critiques in one setting, which can be overwhelming. Sandwiching your criticisms in this way is more constructive and prevents you from being overly harsh when you're angry or in the heat of the moment. When you do need to tell your child how to do something better, avoid "you" statements. Frame your thoughts as "I" statements instead. For example, you might say, "I find it frustrating when this happens," instead of "You always do this and it frustrates me."

Even if your child is cranky, talking back, or flipping out, find something positive with which to start the conversation. Train your mind to know that your child is trying to find her way. Remember that she is having a hard time, not giving you a hard time. This will help you create an atmosphere in which your child will be comfortable asking a question or owning up to a mistake.

Be Your Child's Go-To Person

When your relationship has a solid foundation, your child—even a teen who is seemingly detached and distant—will feel safe coming to you with a question or concern. To your child, you are safety, the person she knows will always be there for her. She knows your love is unequivocal. She can count on you.

You want to continue cultivating your relationship with your children for their entire lives. You plant seeds in the childhood years, then water, fertilize, and care for them as they grow. Sometimes the seedlings need to be propped up a little or weeded, or pests in the garden need to be shooed away, but you as the parent/gardener are always there to tend them carefully and lovingly.

Even if something your child does shocks you, you need to remain nurturing in your approach. Say, for example, your child asks you a question about sex or a controversial subject; react with support, and praise her for coming to you (even if you are surprised or embarrassed). Here are a few examples you can use that are positive in nature:

- "Thank you for asking me."

- "That's a good question!"

- "I'm glad you came to me with this question."

Then go ahead and take a moment to formulate a response. If you need to, take longer. Make sure that you can set aside any personal issues or hang-ups, so they don't get in the way. Everyone gets caught off guard sometimes, but thanking your child for asking the question will demonstrate that you're the one to ask. It also means she'll be more likely to ask you about another important issue in the future.

You don't have to wait for your kids to bring up a subject. If you haven't had conversations with your child about the important issue of sex yet, you need to do so as soon as possible (see chapter 2).

Above all, to become your child's go-to person you need to validate your child—for having questions, for her interests, and for being able to vocalize her desires and needs. This will deepen your relationship with your child. Try hard to bracket any squeamishness about awkward topics. Pay close attention to things that your kids and their friends like (you'll learn more about this in the next chapter). Encourage questions.

Some children ask a lot of questions, and that can get tiring for their parents. But, please, never tell a child that her question is silly or inappropriate, and please don't scold a child for asking a question more than once. Your first reaction might be to get frustrated and assume that your child

doesn't listen, but children will often ask a question several times as they begin to piece together their own understanding. Think of their learning like a picture in a coloring book: The more you color in an area, the brighter and clearer the picture becomes. That is how children learn. Try to be patient and find a different way to explain your answer, or offer more examples of how the topic relates to your child's life.

Never give your child the silent treatment. If a child has stepped sideways and made a mistake, you don't turn off your love. Don't try to make her feel like you must teach her a lesson. Assume the role of a shepherd who is guiding your children and who will never abandon them. When children feel like their parents' love is unwavering, they are much more likely to call on you when they need help— you want to be the one your teen is dialing at one o'clock in the morning when a party goes off the tracks.

Mistakes Will Be Made

Your kids are going to make errors in judgment. When they do, they have to trust that they can call you and you'll be there for them without judgment in their time of need. A teen's 1 a.m. distress call from a party is what you want as a parent! That is what allows you to keep kids safe. They need to know you won't shame, berate, or inundate them with questions. If you have questions or concerns, hold them until the next day when you can have a calm, rational discussion. Any deserved consequences or punishments can usually wait until the next day, too.

Aside from being the most important foundational piece of the parent-child relationship, unconditional love is especially powerful as an antidote to shame. When your child comes to you with a question or to confess something he's seen or done, reacting first with unconditional love will set up an ongoing relationship of trust between you and your child.

When your child knows that he is loved no matter what, that there is nothing he could ask or say or do that would make you question your love for him, he is secure. Security lays the groundwork for healthy self-esteem and strong relationships as your child progresses toward adolescence.

Laying the foundation for a loving relationship with your child will pay dividends, as he will feel comfortable talking to you about anything. This is a critical component in equipping your child to navigate the complexities of an increasingly sexualized teen world. We must convey, portray, and radiate acceptance to our children.

Be careful that you don't confuse positive discipline with punishment.

- Punishment: Parent is judge and jury, and convictions mean punitive measures designed to be as unpleasant as possible, regardless of how they relate to the infraction.

- Positive discipline: Parent and child acknowledge that the child made a mistake and work together to determine the path forward. The child experiences the natural consequences of his choices.

You'll find that natural consequences can be more powerful teachers and deterrents than any imposed punitive actions you or your co-parent will enforce. Using the mistake as a teachable moment will also go a long way toward making sure it doesn't happen again.

Handle Your Own Feelings

It's normal to be a little taken aback when your child comes to talk with you about something you're not prepared for, but if you react too strongly, your child may feel she has done something wrong and regret telling you. If it's a serious situation, or one in which your child made a really bad choice, it can be hard not to fly off the handle. How can we parents learn to control our reactions, so our children understand that they are loved, no matter what?

To use psychological terms, I want parents to consider ways in which they show *emotional reactivity*—a disproportionately intense emotional response—versus ways they show *purposeful authenticity*—an intense reaction that is appropriate to the situation. Another way to describe emotional reactivity is that it is a knee-jerk reaction of exasperation or frustration, such as annoyance when a child spills or drops something. Purposeful authenticity, on the other hand, is a deliberate reaction that may be intense but is used to course-correct or draw attention to a critical infraction. A purposefully authentic reaction comes from an intention to guide your child rather than as a way to vent your own frustrations.

As parents, we need to remember that adage, "Don't cry over spilled milk"; mistakes happen, and we can't get too upset over small ones. A dropped plate. A torn dress. A lost sneaker. Whatever. In the scheme of things, these are such small mistakes! If you react emotionally, these things will get blown out of proportion and your child will not learn a lesson as much as to fear your reaction.

When I was in graduate school, we learned that if a child in a therapy session accidentally spills (or drops) something, the therapist should say, "Sometimes things spill/crack/break." Kids' brains can't keep up with their motor growth, so they are often uncoordinated. Spills happen. Don't make them a big deal.

If you do lose control of your feelings, self-evaluate: What is it that really set you off? Are you tired or stressed? Take responsibility for your reaction. You can apologize to your child and explain why you lost your cool. You don't want to have a child feel like she is walking on eggshells around you for fear of eliciting a bad reaction because that prevents trust. A child who feels safe around you is more able to be her authentic self and develop that important growth mindset that lets her take a mistake in stride.

Regulating our own emotions is hard, but it's something we've all—hopefully—been practicing throughout our adulthood. Projecting negative emotions onto our kids can make them become fearful of a mistake, which erodes confidence and can cause them to question our love.

There will be times in your child's life when she makes a mistake of a serious nature, possibly putting herself or someone else in danger. In these cases, an amplified response from you may be appropriate. Your child needs to realize how serious her choices can be, and a big reaction from you may be just what she needs to learn this lesson. That is purposeful authenticity—it's real, it's reasonable, and it is designed to get results.

So check your words as you respond to a question or a concern your child brings to you about her body or about sex. Make sure not to accuse or use derogatory language. You can say that you imagine what she saw was confusing. Offer basic context so your child understands that the images she viewed aren't realistic depictions of healthy behavior. Also, remind her of your online safety plan (see page 35) and expectations.

Following are strategies you can use in regulating your own emotions. All will help you react in a reasonable way when something concerning happens. Children may not feel they are loved unconditionally if they are worried about a parent flying off the handle every time they make a mistake. By communicating unconditional love, you can create a safe, supportive atmosphere to ensure that your child thinks of you as her go-to person and that she has room to learn lessons from making mistakes. Using these steps, you'll be better able to manage your response and be proactive in your interactions with your child.

THE THREE BS

When a parent starts to feel frustrated, there are three things to remember. I call these the three Bs:

- Be quiet.

- Back away.

- Breathe deeply.

SHAPE BREATHING

A great technique for managing our own emotions and reactions is to use shape breathing. I tell parents to imagine breathing in the shape of a B: Breathe in going up the tall back of the "B," hold your breath going down around the top bump, and then exhale around the second bump.

This can occupy your mind for a few moments while you take deliberate breaths and slow down. Even ten seconds can be enough time to remind yourself to stay calm.

BRACKETING

Bracketing is another strategy I recommend: It means putting your own reactions in a box, so you can focus on your child. Once you deal with what he is experiencing, you can return to your own feelings about the matter. Talk it over with a friend or a counselor, if needed. You may be angry or you may be scared about what this situation means for your child's future, but you put your emotions aside, consider what your child needs from you, and focus on providing that guidance, and only that guidance, for this moment. Remember your reactions have a purpose, and you must be mindful of that at all times.

MANAGE YOUR OWN TRIGGERS

You are human, and you will, from time to time, reach a breaking point that causes you to lose your cool. We all have triggers that make it more challenging for us to respond in a calm and purposeful manner. Managing your own triggers is essential when you're parenting. To do that, be realistic and practice self-care:

1. Give yourself enough time for tasks and appointments so you're not always racing around.

2. Go to bed early so you're rested.

3. Don't let yourself get too hungry.

4. Ask yourself what sets you off and how you can avoid those situations.

5. Set yourself up for success.

Shame

To talk about shame, we'll return to the story of William and his daughter, Sonia, who reenacted a scene from a hardcore pornographic video she accidentally saw online at age ten. Sonia's recovery took some time, but William's meaningful support of his daughter's psychological and emotional needs made all the difference for her.

First and foremost, William offered meaningful support and unconditional love to his daughter. He did not embarrass, humiliate, scold, or discipline her. When he realized something was wrong, he bracketed his own emotions and didn't let the situation trigger him. During the months following the incident, William struggled to react in appropriate ways to the fallout and to make decisions that were right for Sonia. He also reached out for professional help immediately. He did not let pride or embarrassment stop him from talking openly with a therapist or with his daughter, as uncomfortable as it must have been. Sonia did need, and received, regular psychotherapy for several months.

William was also excellent at building a relationship with his daughter. Because it had always been just the two of them, they already had a solid relationship, but William doubled down on this effort. Having a job where he could work from home was extremely beneficial, and he made the most of it. He flexed his hours so that he could walk Sonia to school each day, be there when she got home, and have dinner with her every night.

Even as Sonia's friendships started to suffer because of outside forces, William and Sonia became stronger. It wasn't always perfect, of course. Sonia, like every child growing into a teen, developed an attitude and started pulling away from her dad. But amid these normal emotional growth patterns, they kept up the traditions they'd started during therapy— William at home after school and dinner together—which served as steady bookends for their relationship. William kept the dialogue open on every subject, made sure he was there for Sonia when she wanted to talk, paid attention when she didn't, and brought up uncomfortable issues to normalize those conversations.

Sonia was able to move past her disturbing experience and its aftermath, and has grown into a happy and healthy young adult, due in no small part to her father's absolute commitment to her recovery, his ability to shield her from shame, and his unconditional love.

***

Every parent loves his child unconditionally, but being intentional and thoughtful about building a foundation of love, trust, and openness fosters a positive relationship that lasts throughout the adolescent years and beyond. Some crucial psychological effects flow from a parent's unconditional love, including emotional intimacy, empathy, resilience, and healthy relationships.

You are your child's biggest influence, whether or not you feel that. A parent's love and protection will have the greatest impact on a child, so maintaining a strong bond should be the focus of your purposeful parenting. Validate your child's feelings and needs, and allow for his curiosity. Nurture a growth mindset. Be sure to regulate your own reactions. Understand that your child will make mistakes. Childhood is never free from struggle, but remember that your child is navigating what may be the most complex developmental landscape in history, and that some of those challenges can be serious.

We've looked at the first two points on the Compass: Start Early and Give Unconditional Love. Next up is Stay Current, a must for parents in today's tech-obsessed world.

I noticed that you came back from Rebecca's last night with a whole bunch of makeup on. You looked really pretty.

Yeah, it was really fun! We did it with Rebecca's older sister.

Yes, you looked very beautiful, however I thought that maybe it was TOO much makeup. The way that makeup works is that you wear it light and natural during the day, and maybe put on a lot for a dressy occasion.

I didn't know there were different types of makeup for day and night!!

Ha! Ha!

I'd really like for you to learn how to do makeup properly. How about for your next birthday we could go to the makeup counter and the lady can show you how to put it on so it's not overdone?

That sounds really fun! Let's do that.

How did your parents demonstrate unconditional love? What will you do the same and what will you do differently?

_____

_____

_____

_____

_____

_____

_____

_____

_____

_____

_____

_____

_____

_____

_____

_____

_____

_____

_____

_____

_____

_____

_____

How do you currently show your child unconditional love?
What three other things could you do to demonstrate this?

_____

_____

_____

_____

_____

_____

_____

_____

_____

_____

_____

_____

_____

_____

_____

_____

_____

_____

_____

_____

_____

_____

_____

_____

_____

_____

_____

_____

_____

_____

4

CHAPTER 4

STAY CURRENT

As parents, we all have a lot going on in our daily lives and a variety of demands on our time—work, spouse, kids, schedules, and so on. It can be hard to stay on top of our own workload, never mind our kids' latest interests and activities. It's easy to assume that the apparent absence of a problem means there aren't any. When something troubling *does* occur, it can catch us by surprise. Dealing with an unexpected problem can be tricky because you must simultaneously get up to speed on the causes of the problem and decide how to best handle it.

You'll have an enormous advantage in steering your kids clear of trouble if you stay current with what's going on in your children's world, especially trends that attract teens: the popular social media, videos, music, brands, specialty items, and games. Even if you think your children are too young, aren't interested, or don't have access to the latest fad, you need to know about it because, sooner or later, every child will hear about the next big thing from a classmate at school, try it at a friend's house, or see it online. Parents need to get on top of even innocuous trends early so they are better prepared when more troubling issues, such as drugs or other risky behaviors, do come along.

This means checking in regularly on what your child does online and on social media. For any age group of children, you must know what they are doing, what their friends are doing, and who is influencing them. Although some of the details of technological advances or social media interactions may be confusing, you need to know enough to be able to monitor your kids' use of these apps or platforms.

This chapter is less about policing and controlling your child than it is about staying connected to what *matters* to your child and being aware of the world around him. You want to know what kids are talking about in school hallways and locker rooms. Learning their interests allows you to do a little research and then discuss those activities with your child, as needed. If a problem crops up later, you're more likely to have already had a foundational conversation on which you can build to discuss the specific situation at hand. And, if you're aware of a trend, you're less likely to be caught off guard.

Why You Need to Keep Up

Staying current in your child's life is an investment of time and energy, and offers one more way to build a solid foundation for your relationship. When a parent is meaningfully connected and engaged, the child knows he is a priority. When that bond is absent or lacking, a child will try to get it back, sometimes by doing things to get attention. Those attention-seeking behaviors can ramp up if the attention he is looking for doesn't arrive, and a child may start to do things that are more shocking or provocative, simply because it gets him the reaction—attention—he desires.

So spend time listening and observing. Follow up so you really get to know and understand your child. The conversation needs to go deeper than asking for a quick rundown of his day or a Christmas/birthday list. Your attention needs to go deeper than showing up for dance recitals or soccer games. You must really get to know your child—his interests, his hopes, and his friendships.

Parents should aim to participate in their child's world without becoming helicopter parents—hovering constantly—or making their kids feel like they are living in a police state—surveilling relentlessly and always suspicious. Rather, you want to immerse yourself in your child's life on a regular basis, taking a deep dive into his world to understand what is important to him—and who is important to him. You can come up for air a bit, stepping back a little to give him room but remaining present, and then dive back in when an opening to learn more presents itself. Prioritizing your time so that you are plugged into what matters is what really resonates with your child.

When it comes to sexual issues, you may be surprised to see how much innuendo makes its way into the consciousness of our youth, particularly when it comes to gender roles. Parents should be aware of sexualized themes in video games, song lyrics, movies, TV shows, and toys. It can be helpful to sit down with your child and watch a movie or play with a toy alongside him and have a critical discussion about themes you notice that seem problematic.

Here are some questions you could ask to draw attention to the topic:

- "Wow, did you ever notice that this movie only shows boys liking math or science and girls liking classes like English and music? That's not how it is in real life!"

- "I know you like playing your cousin's video games, and this one has really great graphics, but I don't like the way it talks about girls and women. We both know this isn't real, but it really bothers me."

- "The boy on that TV show seemed like he wanted a girlfriend so bad that he didn't care about the kind of person she was, but she's pretty mean to his friends. I wouldn't want a girlfriend who acted like that, no matter how good-looking she is. And I'd tell her that she can't treat my friends that way, either!"

In commenting on everyday examples of sexism and portrayals of gender, you can draw your child's attention to two things: 1) the inequities surrounding gender that are sometimes taken for granted in our society, and 2) that what these media outlets depict isn't always aligned with reality. It is important for children to learn this type of savvy media consumerism, so they learn to question messages that don't reflect your family's values rather than taking what they see at face value.

Balancing Their Right to Privacy and Your Need to Know

Parents often worry about being overbearing and wonder, "Where is the line between staying current and surveilling my kid? Should kids have *any* privacy?" The answers to those questions can only come from you and your family. Some parents pride themselves on supervising their kids stringently, while others prefer to be more relaxed with the rules until there's a problem. In either case, as long as you are imparting the values of your family in a loving, consistent manner and taking into consideration the individuality of your child, you'll find the right balance.

Even if you decide that you want to keep a close eye, you don't want to become Big Brother, watching over every single thing your child does every hour of every day. Trying to control what kids do is like herding cats— impossible! They're going to be going in all directions. Your child is going to read that explicit magazine or check out that website out of pure curiosity. He's going to try to find ways around your rules. All of this is normal behavior for kids.

If you have some semblance of control through strictness, you need to think about whether your children will be able to maintain such control over themselves when they are out of your sight and making decisions on their own. Additionally, please consider whether they are chafing under your tight reins so much that they'll be gone as soon as they get the chance to be free of your restrictions. Sometimes, too much control can be harmful. Children really do need to learn from their own mistakes. It's the hardest thing in the world for a parent to do, but it's a good idea to let kids make mistakes and learn from the consequences.

Stepping back and giving kids room to experiment is healthy, but stay generally aware of what they're up to; ignorance of a brewing problem is truly dangerous. You can't stop what you don't know about or are unwilling to see. Watch for signs that you may need to react to your child's behavior. Such warning signs include your child:

- Responding to questions in a consistently vague or evasive manner

- Sleeping too much or too little

- Gaining or losing weight rapidly

- Spending more time than usual in their room/alone

- Dropping longstanding or healthy friendships for newer ones

- Making any kind of drastic alteration to appearance (such as cutting all their hair off)

- Showing a high level of irritability

- Using the Internet in middle of night or at odd hours; slamming a device closed or hiding the device when discovered

Monitor kids' online activity, but don't lock them down so hard that they can't participate in normal activities with their peer group. As much as we may want to keep our children in a bubble, that's impractical. Instead, the points of the Parental Compass, when put in practice, create a protective layer that absorbs many of the blows struck by the outside world.

The Parental Compass is intended to replace the need for a rule book—because so many things are coming at our kids these days, one set of rules doesn't work anymore. Besides, technology changes so fast that much-used platforms are constantly abandoned for newer ones, usually just at the point when we parents feel we understand them. Rules are important, but by using the concepts that underpin each point in the Compass, you are building a bond with your child that allows you to be an inextricably connected participant in his life—and that connection makes you better able to keep him safe from harm.

Become a Nimble Parent

One of the keys to parenting effectively in an increasingly sexualized world is being able to respond appropriately and quickly to any issue that concerns you. You can best do this if you're up to date on the risks, trends, and dilemmas that children are facing. Look two to four years ahead of your eldest child's age, as some likely influences are older kids in the neighborhood or friends' older siblings. This look ahead is about staying informed—remember, knowledge is power! Keeping on top of trends—even when you think, "We're not there yet"—means you are less likely to be caught by surprise if or when your child does become involved in certain trends or behavior. Staying aware is about tucking information away in your mind so you know what you'll be dealing with even before it occurs.

Continuing our in-depth look at stories from my clinical practice, I want to share two cautionary tales. Nathan and Emily are extreme examples of the dangers that can befall children when their parents don't stay on top of risks facing tweens/teens. Desensitization to sexual or violent images or videos is now a scourge. Unfortunately, this type of content has saturated too many areas of children's lives, including social media and online videos.

Inappropriate content has become normalized. Too many people are confusing what they see in these images with what takes place in real life. This confusion affects adults, but it has an even greater effect on teens, who already have a hard time understanding the real world.

Nathan's Story

Nathan, like many kids, loved playing video games. Early in elementary school he started playing age-appropriate games, but he was always enthralled with his older brother's games. His parents started off prohibiting the games meant for a more mature audience, but as the years went by they became less stringent with those rules. Meanwhile, Nathan

slowly began to lose interest in other activities.

Never an athletic boy, Nathan had played soccer and baseball for a while, but his own middling abilities and a team record with more losses than wins left him unmotivated. This smart kid's academics were good but he was often bored in class because he learned so fast. In video games, he found an exciting environment where he excelled. At eight and nine years of age, Nathan loved building virtual worlds and mastering all the hidden tricks in a game. When he progressed to multiplayer games, he found that he was more successful than he'd ever been on the baseball field.

Video games boosted Nathan's self-confidence. Self-confidence is a foundational characteristic upon which much else is built, including a positive self-concept, social skills, self-efficacy, optimism, and a willingness to try new challenges. Every child should be able to find something he is good at and be able to engage in that activity for fun and also for an ego boost.

At this point, Nathan's mom took a new job a thousand miles (1,600 km) away and the family moved. Nathan didn't have an abiding interest in baseball and so didn't sign up in his new town. Not knowing anyone, Nathan came home after school and played games online with his friends from his old town, just like they always had done. He increasingly spent time alone, but he was interacting with friends he'd had for a long time so his parents didn't worry. Busy with new jobs, Nathan's parents started slacking on monitoring his online activities.

When Nathan was ten, his sixteen-year-old brother started playing first-person shooter video games that were more exciting than Nathan's building games. He begged his brother to teach him, and then started playing on his own. Nathan quickly mastered the shooter games and looked for new ones to play. One day, he was on his brother's computer looking for a new game and came across something different: a video, something he'd never seen before. It was pornography, and he was confused but instinctively knew it should be kept a secret. He watched the video many times, surreptitiously, and one day he found another one to watch.

His parents were still pretty hands-off, not realizing what their son was accessing online. Nathan seemed stable, and though he was in the house much more often than before, there were no problems cropping up, so they left him to his own devices. They figured he was still adjusting to the move and would get more involved with school and friends when he was ready.

Nathan played mature video games incessantly because he had gotten to the point where he'd become

desensitized to the violence they portrayed. Repeated exposure to a stimulus (in this instance, violent imagery) lessens the emotional response that would normally take place. Once Nathan was desensitized to the thrill of video games, he sought a new kind of stimulation: pornography.

By the time he turned eleven, Nathan had developed a porn habit that manifested itself in his attitude toward girls in school. He couldn't distinguish between what he saw on the screen and what was appropriate in real life, so on several occasions he approached a girl and insinuated some graphic sexual desires. He thought they would like it, like the girls in the videos. He'd been conditioned to think that sex acts happened casually, and at the mere suggestion of a male.

Additionally, having been desensitized to violence and sexual material, Nathan lacked the capacity to understand the girls' emotional response to his inappropriate behavior. He believed his behavior to be normal, because he had no healthy context for sex or understanding of sexuality. These are the things you can begin to cover (in early childhood) during those conversations about bodies, personal space/bubble (which lays the groundwork for consent), and boundaries (which we'll look at more in the following chapter). Because of his young age, Nathan was also not ready to unpack/contextualize the graphic portrayals of intimate adult behavior he was viewing. His problems stemmed from a combination of too much sexual content too soon, with not enough groundwork.

The girls—and their parents—understandably took offense and reported him to the school, as well as to law enforcement. Police questioned Nathan and his parents, who were shocked, to say the least. This was their first indication that something was amiss with their son, and being informed of his behavior by the police was a huge wake-up call. They contacted my office the next morning and brought Nathan in that afternoon.

As a psychologist, I start to establish a rapport with my patients by explaining that I am a safe, neutral person and that our discussions are confidential. I don't tell a child's parents everything we discuss in our sessions. I also explain that I spend nearly every day researching, writing, and talking with patients about sex and sexuality so *nothing* embarrasses me. I've probably heard every question they could think of to ask, so if they have one, they should go ahead and ask it.

The main points I made in counseling with Nathan, which you can also use or amend for use with your child if needed, are the following:

- Sexuality is natural and it is perfectly normal to be interested in sex and have questions about it.

- Young teens are in a normal phase of life when hormones are on overdrive, so sexual feelings are stronger and more confusing now than at any other point in life.

- Pornography is an industry, designed to keep people coming back over and over again with fantasy-type images—and that sex never happens like that in real life.

- One of the main things that draws people to pornography is that those videos never show people being rejected. How nice would it be to never be rejected and to always have someone say yes to everything you ask? Real life does not work that way.

- Sexual intimacy is most enjoyable when there is a relationship established and a great deal of emotional intimacy prior to sexual intimacy. All of this takes time.

- Boys need to know that most girls will not respond favorably to suggestive comments. These are only appropriate within an emotionally intimate relationship.

- Everyone has his or her own personal boundaries (which we'll discuss in the next chapter), and talking with anyone the way people talk to each other on pornographic videos is a huge boundary violation and can even feel like harassment to the person at whom the comments are directed.

Emily's Story

Expectations about girls' sexual behavior is not relegated to boys who have a pornography habit. There are plenty of girls who come to believe that sex is expected of them, and who act on those beliefs, even to their own detriment. Emily was one of these girls.

Emily desperately wanted to fit in when she started high school. At age fourteen, she acquiesced to the whim of the first boy who expressed interest in her, and soon got a reputation among all the boys. She equated popularity with sexual activity, and many of the boys in her school were happy to take advantage.

Emily wasn't alone in her actions; other girls were doing the same, so she confused sexual empowerment with sex as a commodity that could be exchanged for acceptance and popularity. She was too young and immature to know the difference. From oral sex at the movie theater, Emily quickly progressed to having intercourse between classes at school. That was when an adult finally became aware of the situation and raised a red flag.

When Emily came to see me, she jokingly told me her thighs were actually calloused from having so much sex. She described having almost an "out-of-body" experience when she was having sex, like she was outside the scene watching herself. In psy-chology, this is what we call depersonalization, which is the mind's way of distancing itself from behaviors that it knows subconsciously are traumatizing. This was a way for Emily to feel numb about what was happening to her body, which, at her age, she didn't truly understand. That feeling of watching her body from afar made her feel like she was going crazy.

We spent a great deal of time talking about society's expectations in the realm of sexuality. Many of my clients over the past decade have made it clear that teens today don't equate oral sex with intercourse. Emily underscored this point, explaining that, for her, performing oral sex on a boy was extremely commonplace. A boy would text her and ask her to meet him somewhere, and she'd just go. She'd never had a boy perform oral sex on her, though.

We focused a lot on the idea of sex as part of a pleasurable partnership between two people—preferably adults—who express their love physically. We talked about consent, and that girls don't have to do everything a boy wants them to do. Girls have a right to say no to anything they are uncomfortable with, and they have a right to expect love and tenderness in any physical or emotional relationship.

The hardest part for Emily was to untie the association of sexual activity with popularity and acceptance by her peer group. She said girls who refused sex were "blacklisted" at her school and were sometimes cruelly taunted. The connection was so ingrained in her mind that it was never completely erased, and we spent many counseling sessions giving her coping mechanisms for her anxiety about popularity.

When she entered high school, Emily was unfortunately vulnerable for a number of reasons, some of which the Parental Compass could have mitigated. She didn't have a foundation for her family's values when it came to sexual activity, and she was very naive in terms of her sexual knowledge. She jumped into sex acts quickly, as well. The Start Early point of the Compass would have been helpful because Emily would have had a foundation of knowledge about sex and an understanding of her family's expectations surrounding behavior; this foundation could have guided her away from using her body as a bartering chip to gain popularity.

It is Stay Current that perhaps could have interrupted Emily's fast-track progress to sexual promiscuity. Hindsight is always twenty-twenty, however, Emily's parents needed to be more informed about their daughter's life, as well as about trends and issues affecting young people today. Emily, her parents, and I spent a great deal of time talking about leaving past mistakes in the past and moving forward without blame or shame.

I worked extensively with Emily on power dynamics and using her own willpower. Above anything else, I wanted her to understand that every girl has choices when confronted with sexual situations, and that girls might make different choices at different times in their lives. We also spoke about the thoughts that automatically swirled around in her brain when a boy made a suggestion, emphasizing that saying yes all the time is not sexual empowerment.

Dangerously Desensitized

Both Nathan and Emily had become desensitized and numb to matters concerning their sexuality. The two sets of parents, with help, worked to counteract the deep psychological effects that early exposure to sexual imagery or situations had on their children. Together, we were able to explain the difference between sex and intimacy to these children, and to build up their capacity for an intimate, healthy relationship.

Nathan's and Emily's stories are both extreme examples of the dangers posed when parents don't stay current with their children's activities, online and off. Issues can come up so quickly after exposure to sexual behavior that parents need to be as plugged in as possible.

When parents and kids struggle to connect around awkward topics such as sexuality, outside resources can sometimes help by providing a framework for discussion. My company, FamilySparks (familysparks.com), offers online courses about sexuality that any parent or preteen/teen can watch. In addition to information that will help you talk to your teens about sex, the courses include tips, resource lists, and activities. Jumping into these sensitive conversations with your kids will help you notice when they aren't responding emotionally in a healthy or productive way.

The bottom line is that desensitization to the point where the child experiences a void in his natural emotional responses can be like an insidious cancer, infecting other aspects of his life and leading to additional problems. This is what happened with Nathan, but his example is not an isolated one.

How to Stay Current

It's one thing to know you need to stay current in your child's life, but it's quite another to figure out how to stay on top of trends that change at the whim of an amorphous society of teenagers. There's no simple, foolproof way to do this; parents just need to remain aware and plugged into their kids' lives, their community, their local news outlets, and their schools. You can ask your child:

- "Have you seen anything lately on your phone, the computer, or at a friend's house that made you worried or uncomfortable, or that you thought was inappropriate?"

- "What show is everyone loving these days?" (Then watch the show or research it online.)

- "If you could snap your fingers and be at any concert or music festival right now, which one would it be?" (Then listen to that music, look up the festival, and so on.)

- "What's the best thing about being a [X-year-old] right now? What's the scariest thing?" (Listen to your child's responses, and write them down so you can keep them in mind.)

- "What do you admire most about [new friend you as parent may be having concerns about]?" (This neutral question can clue you into what is attracting your child.)

Talking with your child about concerns you have about her current interests (for example, information you may have learned based on the conversation starters above) may be more effective than banning the worrying content outright. That being said, don't be afraid to enforce your own standards if your children are offered toys or clothing, or are asked to attend events, that you feel are inappropriate. It's okay to say, "We're not ready for that."

We have covered screening for potential risks, but how can you encourage the content and activities you *are* comfortable with? Staying current on your kids' interests helps you do that, too. Talk with them about what they like to do, and then make the activities you want to encourage easy and rewarding for your kids. For example, if your daughter is really into building with LEGO, think about getting a great new set for a birthday or holiday. Working on it together can be a wonderful bonding experience! If your child starts playing a new sport, go outside and practice together in the backyard before tryouts. If your son gets interested in music during a summer camp, take him to a special concert or sign him up for lessons.

The same approach goes for other popular trends. When your daughter wants to use a new type of social media, try out the platform with her. If your child becomes interested in an online video series or pop star, watch or listen together. If your son is begging for the latest brand of shoes, ask him to show you why he thinks they are so cool (he'll likely bring up a celebrity who wears them, and you can then discuss that celebrity's image). If your child is always asking for a certain specialty item, such as a food or accessory, or to download the latest online game, search the item's name with the keywords "teens" or "what parents need to know" so you can find out the specifics before agreeing to it.

Here are some important additional ways to stay current:

STAY IN THE LOOP AT SCHOOL

Most schools will let you know if there are dangerous trends happening that you need to be aware of. Read the school newsletters and make sure you cultivate a personal relationship with your child's teacher and/or school administrator. Volunteer at the school when you can, or take a morning once a semester or so to go in to school and be available to help, while also being a fly on the wall and learning what you can about your child's peer group.

Most schools offer reproductive education in the elementary and middle school curriculum. You may wish to ask your child's teacher what is being taught and review the material so you are on the same page if your child comes home with questions.

HAVE BOOKS IN YOUR HOME

Sometimes questions crop up at unexpected times. Having some relevant, up-to-date resources about sexuality on hand can be valuable when you're faced with questions. You can also make these books accessible to your child if she wants to look at them on her own.

If your relationship with your child isn't as open as you'd like, don't expect the nature of the bond to change immediately now that you've decided you need to perk it up. It may take some time before you both feel comfortable talking openly about topics related to sex. If that is the case, leaving books around could be a nice way to gently say to your child, "I'm paying attention and I know you want the information but don't want me to make a big deal out of it."

WATCH WHAT GOES INTO YOUR CHILD'S BRAIN

Pay attention to the media your child is consuming. It's not always easy, but make an effort to know what your kids and their friends listen to, watch, and play with—songs, movies, and video games. When your child is interested in adolescent content, such as a PG-13 movie, you'll have to decide whether you believe she is ready for it. If you have watched the movie yourself and are comfortable with it, you'll be able to prepare your child for anything she may see or debrief with her afterward.

If you're at a point where you want to give your child a bit more responsibility (and you don't have time or funds to preview the movie yourself), perhaps it's time to trust that she can handle whatever might be included. I'd suggest having a conversation with her before she goes and another after she returns. Here are some ways to start that conversation:

- "What did you think of that movie?"

- "Would it be okay for a younger student to watch?"

- "Can I recommend the movie to other families?"

- "Did that movie bring up any questions for you?"

- "So what rating would *you* give it?"

Another way to learn about what your child and his friend are interested in is to simply listen to them talk during carpool. If your kids are like mine, they forget you're even there when their friends are in the car with them. So turn the volume on the music down a bit when they're getting into a conversation so you can overhear the topic and their thoughts. You don't need to say anything or interject at all, just keep your ears open and your eyes on the road.

If you hear anything that concerns you, hold it until you get home and have a private moment to talk with your child. Keep in mind that you may not have heard the whole story. You could say, "You know, I happened to overhear you talking in the car yesterday and you said something that made me start to worry a little. Let's sit down and talk about it." Tell him what you thought you heard, without accusation, and then give him a chance to tell you what they meant or explain any relevant context to help you understand.

FIND THE POSITIVE IN SOCIAL MEDIA

Finally, although social media can be a platform where problems occur, it doesn't have to be. There are plenty of ways to use social media tools to become closer to your kids and monitor their activities at the same time. It's also a great place to learn some of their likes and dislikes and to get ideas for birthday presents or special outings. Social media can be a window into your child's soul, and can complement—although it should never take the place of—your face-to-face relationship with your child.

Friending your child or following his accounts might be okay for some kids, though others might be apprehensive. Give him a chance to express his concerns and listen to what he is saying. Is he afraid you will comment too much or embarrass him where his friends can see? Is he worried you'll monitor his every keystroke? Does he have other concerns? Talk with your child about these feelings and honor any promises you make about controlling your own behavior.

***

Staying current in your child's life is one of the most important ways you can provide protection. We parents cannot be there every moment, so we need to make sure kids know how to behave when we're not around. Understanding, establishing, and protecting personal boundaries is another crucial skill our kids need to learn, and we'll explore that in the next chapter, "Set Smart Boundaries."

So, since you've been using that new chat app, what do you think of it?

I like it a lot! It's fun and you can use all those neat filters.

Do you think it would be appropriate for your sister, or your cousin?

I'm not sure. Some of that stuff might be confusing for a younger kid, and sometimes people use bad language.

I think you're probably right. If you could give it an age rating, what would it be and why?

I think for a high-schooler it's ok. By now most of my friends and I have a good idea of what's safe and what isn't.

Set a goal to ask your child at least one of the questions suggested in this chapter. Which one will you choose? What do you hope to learn from the answer?

5

CHAPTER 5

SET SMART BOUNDARIES

Each of us makes decisions about our own boundaries every day. For children, smart boundaries are crucial to development and personal safety. Boundaries are about respect, both for oneself and for others. When children have a clear understanding of their personal boundaries, they are better able to assess situations that make them uncomfortable and are better equipped to know what actions to take when a boundary is crossed.

Every child needs to know that his (or her) personal space is sacred, and that his body should never be touched inappropriately. As parents, teachers, and counselors, we need to teach children a thorough concept of consent so they are able to exude confidence when they tell someone no—a key deterrent to potential predators and abusers. This knowledge is equally important for boys and girls. Children who learn how to set and enforce boundaries also understand how to respect the boundaries of others and what kind of touching is appropriate in a variety of situations.

Boundaries can be crossed by a friend, sibling, or potential abuser. As we will see in this chapter, there are several types of boundaries and a variety of situations in which they can be tested. The crossing of a boundary can mean a number of things. Most alarmingly of course, it could mean that a child is in trouble—either being taken advantage of or being hurt. The crossing of a boundary doesn't always mean immediate harm—it can simply put a child on a dangerous trajectory. Once a boundary is reduced or damaged, it's easier for a potential abuser to cross it again or to cross the next one, and then a child can find herself on a slippery slope.

A fundamental understanding of boundaries is necessary for healthy relationships, family interactions, friendships, social/community conduct, and protection from abuse. A fundamental lack of understanding of boundaries places a child at risk on all of these fronts. This is what I mean by a child being on a dangerous trajectory. For example, a young boy

who is not taught that people have "personal bubbles" may be the boy who snatches toys from other children at age four; gives unwanted hugs, shoves, or other physical contact at age eleven; and then doesn't understand sexual consent as a teen and ends up committing sexual assault.

Similarly, children who do not understand that they can say no to an uncle asking for a hug during a holiday visit may also not understand that they can say no to someone touching their private parts; as they grow, they may become teens or adults who do not say no to a partner who is asking

for something they are not ready to give. These are extreme examples, but harmful outcomes are the reason boundaries matter across the board, even though a specific situation might seem inconsequential.

Concentric Rings

In my practice, I regularly explain the concept of boundaries, not only to parents but to the children I am treating. It's always hard to describe this psychological concept so that children can wrap their minds around the idea of protecting themselves. That's why I developed the Concentric Rings: to help people think about the different ways we interact with those around us and the ways we respect ourselves and our fellow human beings.

Here are the Concentric Rings, and what they mean for each of us.

THE SELF RING

Inside every person is a center, where his or her true self resides. This core is what I call the Self Ring, and it links your heart, your mind, and your gut. Inside this Self Ring are the most important principles of who you are, those core characteristics that make up your moral compass: This includes attributes such as kindness and lessons from parents about traits such as integrity, and can also include religious tenets and sometimes interests of a deep, abiding nature.

Each child's core is different and that's what makes each of us unique and special. The innermost ring is the boundary inside oneself. It explains that feeling you get in your gut when you're thinking about doing something you shouldn't—it's like that ring is giving you a warning from inside. This center ring is about an understanding of, and thus respect for, one's self.

If we're being true to ourselves and respecting ourselves, our actions and words are aligned with the attributes inside our core. Of course, some traits may evolve as we age; a person can learn to adapt to new situations

more easily or to be less self-critical, for example. Tastes and interests can certainly change throughout our lives. Our internal boundaries are there for a reason: When we're stretching that ring too far, we feel it in our gut. This gut feeling when something is not quite right is instinctive and exists to protect us. It's almost like a sixth sense. If we listen to our hearts and minds, we tend to make sound decisions.

Tell your children to listen to their gut, whether they are with you or on their own. That Self Ring is there even when no one is looking. When it comes to that core, your child should make no compromises. A person is not being rude or selfish when she is being true to herself. Self-respect, after all, is the cornerstone of self-esteem. Parents, think back to a time that you made a decision by following your gut, and explain your decision-making process to your child. Modeling this type of decision making is a powerful lesson.

To develop boundaries, you have to know what your values are and where the line between right and wrong stands. It's important that your child knows who you are and what you believe. Because kids will not be able to define their own boundaries for themselves until they are older, they need to know unequivocally *your* boundaries; when they are younger they will use your boundaries as models for their own. This means you must communicate your personal values and stick to them. If you value honesty, for example, then talk about its importance in your life and live that value day to day. Kids are guided by watching what you do, which often makes a bigger impression than what you say.

Staying true to oneself is an ongoing lesson for all of us, so don't be surprised when you have to keep reinforcing the boundaries of the internal ring to your child. This is an exercise in modeling how you, as a parent, live according to your own moral values, to encourage your child to search herself for similar guidance from within. This means that you must walk your talk: It could be apologizing to the police officer if you get a speeding ticket, instead of getting defensive, or it could mean giving up your bus seat to an elderly person and whispering to your child why you did it. It means telling the truth.

And you must model boundaries across the board, so your child sees them in action. For example, you can share, "I don't like that show because the characters spend a lot of time making fun of that boy, and I don't think that is kind." Or you might ask, "May I please post this picture of you in your Halloween costume onto my [social media platform] profile? It's important to me that you give permission before I share a picture of you." Make sure, also, that you give your child room to establish her own internal ring, which may or may not be exactly the same as yours. Parents are the greatest influence on a child's inner core, but they are not the exclusive factor.

THE FAMILY RING

The next ring in the Concentric Rings concept is the one that encompasses family. It is within this Family Ring that we teach children how to respect others and how to insist on respect *from* others. Your individual family situation determines who is included in this ring, but certainly those family members who live in the same household have a place there, and perhaps also close family who live nearby and are in your child's life on a regular basis.

The boundaries of the Family Ring are about love and respect. The Family Ring represents the bond between people who love one another and will always protect and nurture one another. These are the people your child is closest to in the world, even if there's some sibling rivalry or friction with parents from time to time. You come up with your values as a family, together. If one of your principles is "respect" and your son is frequently rude to you and calls you names, let him know the consequence he can expect from you each time that happens. Let him see that you respect yourself and will follow through. This is different from trying to "make him" speak the way you want him to. You're giving him the choice but you're holding him accountable.

THE COMMUNITY RING

Outside the Family Ring is the ring for the larger community in which you live. This consists of other family members who may not be as close geographically or emotionally, as well as friends, classmates, teachers, teams, and coaches. In short, the Community Ring includes those people you interact with in person on a semiregular basis. The caveat "in person" is an important one: People your child knows IRL—in real life—must be differentiated in today's world from those she may know or interact with in an online capacity only.

Boundaries in the larger Community Ring should be fairly strict and enforced. Although every family's rules will be different, a common example would be that your child can't get into anyone's car without express permission from you or unless the person uses an emergency code word you've established. Certainly expectations of your child's behavior at school or in a local club or on a team will fall into this category: doing homework on time, showing good sportsmanship, treating teachers and coaches with respect, and honoring commitments to friends. The Golden Rule of "treat others as you want to be treated" is the way many of us describe the expectations within the Community Ring.

Parents should expect children to bump up against many of the Community Ring boundaries on a fairly regular basis (how else do they learn?)

and understand the need to repeat the lessons of these boundaries quite often. From knowing how to behave at friends' houses to following school rules to staying off a crotchety neighbor's lawn, children have a great deal to remember.

There are situations that could tempt a child who doesn't completely grasp the importance of doing the right thing even when no one's watching. Such situations underscore the reasons for defining that inner Self Ring and putting those moral values into practice in the community context—for example, not laughing along with people who are making fun of somebody, not taking an extra cupcake from the tray at school when no one is looking, or not drawing graffiti in a bathroom stall even if nobody will know it's you.

Because there are so many variables, some boundaries within the Community Ring may not be things you can warn your kids of in advance. You need to be as proactive as you can by making sure kids understand basic etiquette and the behavior expected at places they frequent—such as the library or the movie theater, for example—but they must also understand that you can't think of everything and they will have to exercise their best judgment at times. Keep in mind that it's often by bumping into or breaking rules that children learn where the boundaries are in their community.

In all this talk of personal and societal boundaries, you also need to teach your child to respect other people's rings. To be an honorable person is to keep a friend's confidence, to obey the rules at the neighbor's house, and to not push someone to abandon her core values. You and your child should expect this of all her friends, as well.

THE ONLINE RING

Last, there's a ring around the entire earth that encompasses the billions of humans in our global society. In earlier generations, this ring wouldn't have been so important to teach children about because there weren't many ways for them to interact with the world as a whole. Today this is an *extremely* important ring to discuss with your children, as the instant they get Internet privileges, this Online Ring becomes real and accessible. As with many advances in technology, there are both positive and negative ramifications to online information and connections, so your kids need boundaries for their interactions with the big, wide world.

The boundaries of this Online Ring need to be explained to *every* child who uses a computer, phone, smart device, or nearly any piece of tech equipment these days—even if that use is supervised. The online safety plan discussed in chapter 2 is an excellent place to start when it comes to defining online boundaries. These boundaries will be the basis for whatever tech rules your family decides are right for your household. Although a rule might be that your child has to use the computer in the living room instead of his own room, the boundary that needs to be explained is that he should never share any identifying information about himself—full name, address, school name, or even town/state/province (you may wish to explicitly add this to your family's online safety plan). Even the youngest of children needs to know the difference between a friend in the neighborhood and someone who says they're a friend or a peer online.

Children who use the Internet also need to understand your expectations about what they should post and what they should refrain from posting. They especially need to know to avoid sharing their every feeling or the intimate details of their lives. It's sad to say, but there are people who will use that kind of information to take advantage: An online predator may capitalize on it and use it to try to bond or connect, and then exploit that vulnerability; a bully may consider the information fodder for more targeting or teasing.

Personal details should most likely stay in the Family Ring. Discourage children from posting anything deeply private or sensitive online via social media, text, and so on, even if it's to a friend or relative. Private conversations about personal topics are best saved for face-to-face interactions; you would not want your child to accidentally click a wrong button and send a private message to the wrong person or place. It is so easy to make mistakes online. Talk with your children about what you want them to think about before they post online, and make sure to stress that anything posted online is there *forever*.

Popularity online—in the form of followers, likes, or ratings—can be just as alluring as hanging out with the cool group on the weekend. The most famous social media accounts are those that push established boundaries, or even eradicate them. It's only natural that impressionable kids want to emulate what they see, what gets the most "buzz" at school, and what their friends are doing. As we discussed in chapter 4, when we talked about staying current, this is why it's essential that parents monitor their children's accounts, even into high school.

Tyler's Story

Tyler was a timid middle schooler on the fringes of the popular group when, for some inexplicable reason, he became the target of a sick joke. Some of the boys created a social media account for a nonexistent girl and had this fake girl become online friends with Tyler. The boys played it up to Tyler, saying how "hot" she was, and then they sent flirtatious messages from the fake account to Tyler on social media. They started daring him to ask the girl for naked photos,

which they—on the other side of the account—kept refusing. The boys goaded Tyler, saying he just had to keep flirting and asking for the photo. Eventually, they used the fake girl's account to message: "I'll show you mine if you show me yours." Tyler sent a naked photo of himself, which the boys then showed to everyone at school. What had begun as a practical joke ended in criminal charges against the boys for distributing child pornography.

Tyler was aware that what he was doing was wrong. His parents had warned him against predators and naked pictures. But they had never thought a young girl would be the impetus for this kind of trouble. In fact, they hadn't thought of anyone creating a fake account and gaining their son's trust. Tyler, unaware that such cruelty existed in the world, much less in his so-called friends, had never considered that the girl he was talking to was anyone other than the person depicted in the profile. His "relationship" with her had given him a confidence he'd never had and the attention of his cool friends just as he was entering puberty, a fragile time for many kids. It took him years to get that confidence back and to trust another girl.

This Online Ring that your child can access requires strict boundaries and watchful eyes—it would be difficult to overstate this point. Though Tyler's story is one that hopefully won't be repeated in your home, it's not uncommon for kids (and even adults) to be taken in by fraudulent online personas or stories. You must make sure your child understands the potential for someone to take advantage of the anonymity of the Internet.

Practicing good judgment with regard to the Self, Family, and Community Rings prepares children to eventually navigate the online world safely. Explain to your child that a momentary surge of online fame isn't worth crossing smart boundaries and the headaches that may come with it. Hopefully, your child never posts or shares inappropriate material and confines his contacts to people he knows, but you as a parent need to stay vigilant. Breaking the boundaries of the rings can be a slippery slope; once one becomes negotiable—or, worse, is not enforced—it's much easier to cross the next one and then the next. Disregarding boundaries can become a habit and can eventually lead kids to unsafe or unhealthy situations.

Their Bodies, Their Choices

Central to the Self Ring is the fact that a child's body is her own. This is an incredibly powerful concept that, to many, may sound simplistic. It is essential for children to be comfortable with their bodies so that they can make good choices and:

- Understand how their bodies work and not be afraid to ask questions about them.

- Know correct physical terminology so that when they hear the terms somewhere else, they will understand the conversation.

- Know what is private and what isn't private.

- Be conscious of other people's bodies and their private areas.

- Have self-esteem and confidence, now and in the future.

- Know what they can and cannot do to each other; what's appropriate for certain ages and what isn't appropriate.

- Express where they are hurt or where there is pain.

- Feel comfortable with who they are (the more they know and understand, the more they are comfortable with who they are as they get older).

- Trust you, their parents/caregivers, through these important conversations.

- Be prepared for the time when they are confronted with a challenging or uncomfortable situation or person.

As we saw in chapter 2, "Start Early," conversations with children about their bodies should ideally start early, even in infancy and toddlerhood, when a child is just learning to speak. Label body parts with their correct names, answer questions, and respect kids' personal control over their bodies. As your child grows into adolescence and young adulthood, the trust and open communication you've built mean he will hopefully continue to come to you for advice, help, and wisdom. The firm boundaries you've given him will also help him relate and respond to other people in his life in healthy, appropriate ways. Even if you haven't yet had explicit conversations about bodies and respect for personal boundaries, you can still build this foundation. Start talking with your child now—it's never too late.

Eradicate People-Pleaser Tendencies

The tendency to please is human nature. Most of us—children and even many adults—want to make those around us happy, and we want to be liked. Trying to please others is only natural and in many cases can be a good thing. Our polite society is based on the premise of following somewhat arbitrary rules, such as putting your napkin on your lap at dinner, holding a door open for others, and raising your hand in class to ask a question.

The tendency to please, when taken to the level that it becomes a strong habit, can spell trouble. Unfortunately, there are many people who will take advantage of this behavior, so you must work to ensure your kids don't become habitual people pleasers, making decisions and choosing actions aimed at pleasing the people around them—whether they are parents, teachers, peers, or others. When we do something to please someone else, we are at risk of disrespecting ourselves.

This can feel a little counterintuitive. Of course you want your child to do what you tell her to do, and many will want their children to do what teachers tell them to do. A people-pleaser mentality can become problematic, or even downright dangerous, if a child starts to make decisions or take actions that go against what the child herself would do if she was not trying to please someone.

There is a difference between following directions from a parent or teacher about chores or classwork and following directions from a person who is leading you astray. Knowledge of this difference is built from a combination of understanding basic body boundaries (good touch, bad touch; private parts), a bond of unconditional love with parents (predators sometimes threaten "your parents will be so mad if you tell them," and if a child senses that she is loved unconditionally, she will be less likely to believe such a threat), and a strong sense of inner/self boundaries (i.e., "listening to your gut," as developed through modeling by parents and repeated practice). All of these things can be taught and instilled starting when children are young. Teach kids that it's okay to ask questions or say no when something doesn't feel right. Here are some ideas you can share with your child to help her say no:

- "No, thank you." (A courteous refusal is always both polite and direct.)

- "Wow, that looks really fun, but I don't want to do that right now."

- "I'm not comfortable with that, and my family has a rule of no naked pictures."

When your son or daughter needs to be *really* blunt:

- "I've already said no. I don't need to explain myself any further."

- "I'm not ready to do what you're asking me to do."

- "I respect myself too much and my family has rules against doing what you're suggesting. If you respect me, you won't ask me to do that."

When it comes to people-pleasing tendencies, consider society's gender stereotypes and expectations, especially if you have a daughter. As women, we are socialized to be pleasant, cooperative, and selfless. This can be a major issue when it comes to girls' development of their sense of self, particularly when they are older and deciding to become sexually active.

Many girls are taught, often indirectly, to put other people before themselves. A high compliment girls and young women often receive from adults is that they are "polite" or "agreeable" young ladies. A young woman needs to know that she shouldn't ever do something she doesn't really want to do or is not ready to do just to be polite. For example, a girl should not be forced to hug every relative, no matter how remote, who visits for a holiday. Some grandparents, aunts, and uncles still think it's okay to trade presents for hugs.

Although a girl might be nice to a boy at school to be polite, she should never kiss a boy to be polite. As she gets older, she should know that continuing to date a boy she doesn't really like just so his feelings don't get hurt is not being true to herself. It's not healthy for her and, in the long run, it's not healthy for the boy either. I want girls to know that it *is* nice to be helpful, selfless, and protective of relationships (whether a friendship or a romance), but no one should ever make another person feel that she has to do something she is not comfortable doing.

The Essential Idea of Consent

Once reserved for college freshmen, consent is an incredibly important concept for kids of all ages to learn—both girls *and* boys. The idea of consent links back to the Concentric Rings, which encompass a sense of self-respect and also respect for others. Your child's body and choices are his own, so it's a natural progression to teach him that he should be asked before his body is touched. If your child has been learning about boundaries throughout his childhood, this concept will make a lot of sense. Young children feel empowered by the ability to grant permission, and a child who knows how to say no will be a step ahead of anyone who seeks to take advantage.

Pediatricians model consent by asking permission before lifting a shirt at children's checkups. You probably don't ask permission for every touch, but asking your child whether he wants his back rubbed when he is sick is one way to incorporate consent into even casual interactions. Sports coaches should ask before they touch a player to show a correct technique, and it is often appropriate (or respectful) for a new friend to ask another whether he wants a hug. When one child asks a friend to borrow something and the friend says no, that statement needs to be respected and honored. These boundaries are foundational to an understanding of consent later in life.

In the past, the idea of consent was stressed with girls nearly exclusively, but it is a concept that both boys and girls need to understand. Boys can be pressured or victimized just as girls are, so they also need to know how to say no to unwanted touching or a sexual encounter. Beyond that, boys and girls need to understand consent so that they grow up respecting the right for anyone to choose, or refuse, to participate in any intimate acts.

The days of boys saying they didn't know a girl didn't want to "go all the way" are gone, and active agreement is necessary for both people who are engaging in sex. Thankfully, the concept and necessity of consent are more widely understood and practiced today, and violators can be held legally accountable. Kids must understand from their earliest years that no means no, and as they grow they must be taught that an enthusiastic yes from your partner is essential before any sexual activity.

Consent is just an extended idea of respect for others, and you've likely already been building up that value in your child. The trick now is to be specific about what consent for touching means and to give kids the words they need to grant or refuse permission.

NO SECRETS = NO PREDATORS

People who pass themselves off as knowing everything can try to exert power over a person who doesn't, and some use that power to take advantage or abuse. Bullies use this tactic all the time. Unfortunately, so do predators. A child who is informed about sex and sexual matters is more protected than one who doesn't understand what's happening.

Before anything sexual is brought up, a predator will often "groom" a child—and this starts with secrets and slowly breaking down boundaries.

Grooming is a conscious act by someone looking to find a child to exploit. One of the well-known facts in psychology is that predators violate boundaries slowly over time. They confuse the child, making boundaries seem fuzzy. This happens to both boys and girls, starting sometimes with innocuous touches such as horseplay, tickling, or wrestling. Predators start by pushing at boundaries that seem less important and then, over time, they move boundaries that are more significant. Therefore, teaching children the importance of boundaries at each level of the rings and remaining firm in your expectations of those boundaries helps the child be strong and safe in the presence of a predator.

Teach children that they should never keep secrets from parents. Explain to well-meaning grandparents who may want to sneak a reward to their grandchildren that they should not ask your kids to keep it a secret from you. Differentiate a surprise from a secret: A surprise is something that is revealed after a short delay, while a secret is supposed to be hidden forever. Parents need to keep kids healthy and safe, so there can't be any secrets.

A child who keeps secrets is a child who can be made to feel shame or guilt or blame, and thus the predator gains even more power. It's a vicious cycle, because the more scared a child is, the more hold an abuser has over him. The way to protect your child and prevent him from falling victim to a bully or a predator is to empower him and make sure he is confident in his ability to say, "No!"

These statistics from Child Rescue Network are staggering:

- One in four girls (25 percent) and one in six boys (17 percent) will be sexually assaulted before they reach adulthood.

- Ninety-three percent of sexually victimized children know their abuser.

- Thirty-nine percent of sexually victimized children are abused by a family member.

- One-third of sexually victimized children are abused by other children.

I don't share these statistics to scare you, although the possibility is certainly terrifying for any parent. Rather, I share the information because knowing that abuse is a possibility, no matter how remote, allows you to take steps to protect your child, inoculate him against exploitation, and make it less likely a predator will choose him. A child who tells his parents what were supposed to be secrets discourages the predator, hopefully early in the process before grooming takes hold. Predators look for kids who will keep the secret.

Some predators groom a child for years before anything sexual takes place. If the child starts to get upset, the predator may resort to threats, such as, "Your parents will be super mad if they know you've been eating candy and drinking soda every day," or "You'll get in trouble for taking your clothes off in front of me."

Children aren't naturally equipped to handle these types of manipulations; they just know they don't want to get in trouble or worry their parents. This is why having conversations with your children about boundaries is important for their safety. Those conversations help your child make good decisions in the face of a suggestion or act that makes his gut feel uncomfortable. He will also be more likely to tell you when something happens if you've been having regular talks about boundaries and appropriate versus inappropriate touching.

Children who know their bodies are their own, who understand that private parts are supposed to remain private, who can say no to anyone who makes them uncomfortable, who understand what sex is, and who don't keep secrets from their parents are children who can enforce the boundaries that surround and protect them.

HAVE THE "OTHER TALK" REGULARLY

The "Other Talk" is the one about online safety. You need to have this talk on a regular basis, starting before you allow your kids access to the Internet and the billions of people who inhabit that Online Ring. The analogy I use with parents is whether they'd allow their child to ride the bus/subway alone. If you wouldn't be comfortable with your child riding the metro alone, she isn't old enough to roam the Internet alone.

From what I see in my practice, a loosening of boundaries has accompanied the increase in children's participation in digital life, and this is deeply concerning. Many parents assume that what happens online doesn't matter as much as what happens in real life. The truth is that, although real life matters much more than online life, we need to banish the idea that it's okay to cross boundaries in your online life because no one can see or is watching. With seven billion people in the world, someone is always watching, and it's crucial that you and your children understand that what you put online can stay there forever.

Deciding the type of online activities and content that are okay for your children is a personal decision, and one that should involve careful consideration. Here are some questions you might ask yourself as you're making these decisions; refer to them as you adapt the rules over the course of your kids' childhood:

- What is our child doing online—seeking entertainment, information, or a little of both?

- What controls do the devices our child will be using have to help us protect him?

- How much online time do we think is appropriate for our child?

- What kinds of offline activities is our child involved in that he gets as excited about? How can we nurture those interests and make sure online activities don't become his only preference?

- When will we prohibit device use? (Example: at the dinner table, at bedtime, while doing homework—at least the entertainment apps, and so on.)

- If kids will be creating social media accounts, what are the rules for use, and who are the trusted adults (parents, aunts/uncles, siblings, etc.) who can engage with them on these social platforms?

In addition to implementing the online safety plan in chapter 2, you can use the great online tool of the American Academy of Pediatrics (AAP) to create a personalized family media plan—the organization offers suggested guidelines on its website (healthy-children.org). Within the AAP's

recommendations is the following: "Have ongoing communication with children about online citizenship and safety, including treating others with respect online and offline, avoiding cyberbullying and sexting, being wary of online solicitation, and avoiding communications that can compromise personal privacy and safety."

Online boundaries will help your children safeguard themselves on the Internet by teaching them how to keep their personal information private, who to interact with and who not to interact with, and that some people online aren't who they say they are and may have bad intentions. Here are some conversation starters you can use to talk to your kids about online safety:

- "Think about the most terrible or embarrassing photo you've ever had taken of yourself being shared with every person you ever meet, *forever*. How would it feel if you could never make it go away? That's what you need to think about before you post something online about yourself or anyone else. Don't post something in anger or to get back at someone, and if anyone ever posts something mean or nasty about you, come and tell me right away."

- "You need to let me know when you want to explore a new form of social media so we can set it up together. Privacy controls are like having a lock on your diary or one on the front door of our house—they are there to safeguard our privacy and make us feel safe. I want to show you how to restrict who sees your information and who can contact you."

- "Because the Internet is full of millions—billions—of people you don't know, it might seem like there's a kind of invisibility cloak covering your online persona, but that's not true. When you post anything online, you never know what's going to happen with that info. What you think is invisible may not really be, so you never want to cross those boundaries you've set for yourself—be kind, be honest, be mindful of your values."

Use mistakes as an opportunity to educate kids further. If your child makes mistakes or breaks your Internet rules, you should certainly express disappointment and assign appropriate consequences, but be careful not to overreact or make consequences so punitive that your child decides not to come to you in the future with a mistake or problem. Remember, the unconditional part of unconditional love is being able to move past mistakes. Allow your child to make his own mistakes, just like you did.

***

The Parental Compass works best when the bond between parent and child is protected and nurtured. Trust is a delicate thing, and you need to demand that your child observe boundaries while also working to understand the underlying reasons a child might cross a boundary. Sometimes those reasons are confusion or defiance, but sometimes a new technology has popped up and your rules don't address some of its features. At other times, the guidelines have been in place for years and have become outdated or obsolete, so be sure to have ongoing conversations about moving through the world safely and the boundaries you might need to put in place as your child matures.

As your child enters into friendships with more people from more walks of life, and eventually starts romantic relationships, her boundaries will guide and protect her, but her heart must still be open to letting people in. The next chapter looks at how to cultivate relationship-building skills in your child, and how to encourage her to cherish and preserve healthy bonds.

I saw that you posted a photo of your brother's room, making fun of how messy it was.

Yeah it was so messy! I got a whole bunch of likes for that, my friends thought it was hilarious.

I can see how that would seem pretty funny, but did you ask him first?

No of course not! He would never have let me do it.

I get why he wouldn't want you to do that.

But remember our family boundaries? We only post about someone if they say it's ok.

Why do you have to make everything such a big deal?

Well it IS kind of a big deal.

It's a boundary issue. You wouldn't want anyone to post a picture of you first thing in the morning! I think you should take that picture down and apologize to your brother.

Ok Dad, that's what I'll do.

How clear are boundaries in your family? Which boundaries do you feel your child respects and which ones do you need to speak with them about?

_____

_____

_____

_____

_____

_____

_____

_____

_____

_____

_____

_____

_____

_____

_____

_____

_____

_____

_____

_____

_____

_____

_____

_____

_____

CHAPTER 6

NURTURE RELATIONSHIPS

The biggest threat in today's digitally enhanced society is the growing absence of intimacy. Our children are staring at their phones or devices all day and increasingly interacting through a digital medium instead of face to face. For that matter, so are some adults. This has to change.

Without an understanding of how to have a relationship in real life (IRL), a person cannot develop a sense of empathy or an ability to sense the world around them. I am not the only child psychologist worried about this; it's a widely held concern. Children can and should develop intimate friendships as precursors to intimate relationships later in life.

Explain to your children how to choose friends, that they need to be wise about who they allow into their lives, and what happens when a friend hurts their feelings. Encourage in-person interactions, including participation in sports, clubs, and sleepovers with friends. Youth groups or faith-based organizations that undertake community service projects and

discuss emotions can also be great. All of these activities will develop a child's self-confidence in dealing with friends of any gender.

Helping your preteen build healthy relationships with friends, classmates, neighbors, and teammates sets the stage for her to develop healthy romantic, and eventually sexual, relationships in the coming years. Learning how to choose good childhood and adolescent friends will help her to choose a partner who is trustworthy when she is ready for sex.

Playdates and Beyond

When your child is young, you probably set up playdates with neighbors or your child's friends from daycare. Your criteria for fostering a friendship might include the two children's closeness in age, the fact that they play well together, or that you get along with the other parents and want to hang out together. No matter the reason, when children are young, their friendships are most often nurtured, if not wholly orchestrated, by a parent.

Eventually children start to choose their own friends. This may start as interest in a playdate with a new friend at school for whom you'll have to track down the parents to make arrangements. Later the children might exchange parents' numbers directly and facilitate the introduction. Of course, as teens, kids find their own friends and make their own arrangements to meet up.

Strong personal relationships are a protective factor for tweens and teens, as the kids most at risk of being lured into unhealthy or even anonymous relationships online are usually seeking to fill a need for acceptance and friendship. There are many ways you can help your child nurture his or her relationships.

CREATE SOCIAL ENGAGEMENTS

Don't wait for your child to ask to have friends over. He may need a little encouragement, as it can be hard to make friends! Buy an extra ticket to a hockey game, invite another family along to a picnic, or have neighborhood people and their kids over for a BBQ. Encourage face-to-face social interaction so your child is able to create meaningful connections with others.

Similarly, if your child has a friend over for a playdate, the kids might need a little help "getting started." The go-to icebreakers that adults have been socialized to rely on—weather chit-chat, news headlines—aren't relevant

to kids, so provide a few fresh ideas for their social toolbox. Keep a few dollar-store craft activities or board games stashed away to bring out if your child and a new friend seem stuck during a playdate. Initiate lively conversations over lunch or a snack by asking an interesting or absurd open-ended question ("What's the strangest animal you've ever seen in real life? Where were you when you saw it?" or "If this food came to life right now, what do you think it would do first?"). Your child will start to learn your technique and may use it himself to start more conversations at school or in other social situations.

LOOK BEYOND BFFS

Mix it up by inviting different people to different events to ensure your child has a diverse group of peers and isn't dependent on just one friend. While there's nothing wrong with having a best friend, and indeed that's a wonderful relationship to nurture, a BFF shouldn't have exclusive rights to your child's friendship. Continually encourage your son or daughter to befriend new kids at school or invite out a person he's never invited before.

Cultural diversity is also important, so open your child up to friendships with children from varied backgrounds. These relationships are valuable, as they promote a worldview that there's room for everyone. Kids who have friends of different backgrounds become adults who are comfortable with diversity.

ENCOURAGE RELATIONSHIPS IN YOUR FAMILY CIRCLE

Are there aunts, uncles, cousins, grandparents, or other relatives who connect well with your child? Strong bonds with other family members can be beneficial to kids as they progress into their teens. Time spent with relatives can be an opportunity to foster growth and independence from your immediate family unit, but your child is still with trusted adults. For example, a few days of vacation at grandma's house or with the cousins, but without mom or dad, can build a child's confidence. A child's extended family can be a powerful influence on him as he's developing and offers an easy and natural extension of mom and dad's protection.

MEET THE PARENTS

Getting to know the parents of your children's friends has many benefits. Maybe you'll make a friend, too! At the very least, you'll have more information about your child's friend and what might be going on in her life that could affect your child. Additionally, it's easier to coordinate playdates if you're in contact with the other adult. If your child is already a tween and starting to coordinate her own social outings, knowing the parents of her friends can give you peace of mind about the decision-making skills of the group as well as assurance that other sets of eyes and ears are watching out for the kids.

FACILITATE EXTRACURRICULAR ACTIVITIES, CLUBS, AND SPORTS

Get your child involved in activities that involve human interaction, such as sports, clubs, or a youth group. Team sports are fabulous for relationship building, but individual sports carry a great many benefits for your child, too. There are dozens of youth organizations, such as Girl Scouts, Boy Scouts, and 4-H, that kids can join, as well as school activities such as choir, student government, marching band, and the debate club. If your son or daughter doesn't care for one activity, try another, but be careful not to let kids bounce from one activity to another so fast that they don't really get to try any of them fully. It's a good idea to agree to a time frame up front and stick with that, so your child learns to fulfill his commitments and has time to create those relationships that could become lasting friendships.

Swap Screens for IRL Relationships

We've all heard the stats around screen time and how much time kids are spending on phones, computers, and tablets. A survey by the Pew Research Center, the results of which were published in a paper titled, "Teens, Social Media & Technology 2018," found the following:

- Smartphone ownership is nearly universal among teens, with 95 percent reporting they have access to one.

- About 45 percent of teens say they use the Internet "almost constantly," which is nearly double the number in the 2014–2015 survey.

- Another 44 percent say they go online several times a day.

- Taken together, these stats mean roughly nine in ten teens go online at least multiple times per day.

Free time spent on these devices (beyond schoolwork, reading, etc.) takes kids away from face-to-face relationships. Parents need to make sure that real-life socializing is not lost to screen time. Encourage your child to hang out with siblings, send her outside to play with friends, or (if you can convince her) get her to do an activity with you. Give her some extra chores around the house if nothing else works.

Regulating screen time will help to ensure that kids don't become consumed by their devices. They need to have time and room for real relationships with their siblings and family, friends and classmates, and the new people they meet in everyday life. Expecting kids to earn their screen time is a strategy that lets parents create reasonable boundaries around time spent in front of screens while empowering the child with responsibility. Here's what I suggest to parents: If a child wants to watch a movie, then she has to do something to earn it. The rate can be one minute equals one minute or any variation that works for your family. So if you have a rate in which one minute of an activity equals two minutes of screen time, and your child practices piano for half an hour, she gets one hour of screen time.

Parents, also take notice of the time *you* spend on screens—are you often on your phone or tablet, or watching TV? You need to model healthy consumption for your kids. They will mimic your actions, whatever they are.

Relationships IRL take work. Help kids learn the skills they need to develop and nurture these relationships with the following ideas.

TEACH FRIENDSHIP

Teach your child the skills of evaluation: Have him look at himself and think about whether he is a good friend to others. A good friend is clear about his own boundaries and respects the boundaries of others. Friends don't talk behind someone's back, gossip, post things online without permission, share others' embarrassing stories, tattle, or break promises or confidences.

Parents need to teach discernment skills, such as thinking about what kind of person would make a good friend. What does your child think about so-called friends who don't show the characteristics he thinks are important in a friend? Talk with your children about the difference between being friendly and being friends. The number-one friendship rule: To *have* a friend, you must *be* a friend. A good friend includes his friends in conversations or play, shares, is able to take turns, asks questions, has your back, tells the truth, is kind, and doesn't brag or always talk about himself. Another great friendship rule that is easy to remember is: If you want to be interesting, be interested.

BUILD EMPATHY SKILLS

When a child learns empathy, she is maturing enough to be mindful of the concerns of others and learning to be less self-focused. Empathy isn't a trait that comes easily to tweens because they're at a developmental stage where they tend to be focused on themselves. So whenever there's an opportunity to understand how someone else might experience a situation—perhaps in the home, to start with—use it.

One example might be a child who goes into her sister's room to borrow clothes without asking. You can take the opportunity to ask, "How would you feel if someone did that to you?" instead of simply saying, "Give that back!" Use the dynamics and situations within your own home to teach your child the skills she will need to be a good friend outside the home. A lot of empathy-building overlaps with the concept of the Self boundary we discussed in the previous chapter—if your child is in the process of defining her own moral compass and values,

she will likely already be considering how actions affect her feelings, and vice versa.

You want children to be observant beyond themselves, take notice of things going on around them in their school and community, and think about what's happening in the wider world. When they ask you about a homeless person on the street, answer their questions with thoughtfulness and honesty. In return, ask your children questions about things they see. You may be surprised by their insight!

THINK THROUGH ACTIONS AND OUTCOMES

Talk with your children about how actions create certain outcomes or affect themselves and others. This is helpful for building empathy and consideration for others, and it's also crucial for self-awareness. Understanding that something he does can have an effect down the road on many people he doesn't even know is a thought-provoking lesson. Every child needs to learn to think about the way he comes across to others. Along with this concept, you want to make sure your child realizes that even actions as small as the words that come out of his mouth have an effect on other people. Eventually, your child will be able to understand that bigger actions can affect large numbers of people and environments. Help your child think through his actions with questions such as:

- "I wonder how Dad felt when you surprised him with that homemade birthday card?"

- "How do you think teachers feel when kids don't finish their homework?"

- "I wonder what it's like to live close to the ocean when there has been an oil spill?"

- "Why do you think those people are protesting outside that government building?"

Problem Solve Like a Pro

Teach your child how to resolve conflicts rather than just letting a friendship go. Keep in mind that conflicts often arise during times of transition. Many children come into my office to talk through ways to solve a problem. I tell them, "Take a deep breath and then think your way through the problem one step at a time." Here are the steps I coach kids through:

- First of all, what happened?

- Next, how did it make you feel?

- Now let's switch our perspective and pretend we are the other person—what do you think the other person is feeling?

- Next, what do you value about this person/friendship?

- Finally, is there a way to find common ground or a solution that works for everyone? (Take turns choosing the game at the next recess or agree that we won't talk about each other in a mean way to others. Does someone need to apologize? Do both need to apologize and forgive?)

We need to start teaching kids how to compromise, how to ask for forgiveness, how to work through problems, and how to look at situations from another's perspective. Good relationships are worth the investment, and give and take is essential to making these relationships work. Parents can also model these ideals—watching you constructively resolve disputes with your spouse or older children in the family will help your child develop similar skills.

DEAL WITH A BULLY

A bully situation is one that includes intimidation or sustained threats to cross one of the boundaries we discussed in chapter 5. Perhaps the bully is crossing a personal boundary by being unkind or encouraging a child to violate one of her own core values in order to prove something. Kids need to learn to recognize when boundaries are being crossed, have the confidence to say no, and tell a trusted adult. All children need to also learn to respect the boundaries established by other people.

Kids should know that even someone they think is a friend might not act like it at times. This could be a one-time thing, or the other child could be going through a difficult time. In situations like these, kids need to know how to communicate their feelings and explain where their boundaries are. It's important that they try to come to a resolution, which could mean working out the problem with the friend or perhaps going in different directions for a time.

DISCOURAGE EARLY ROMANCES

If your child has a budding interest in romance or dating, he will likely soon face some of the drama that comes along with that. Just as certain friendships include tension, early romantic relationships can be full of angst. A nine-year-old might have the interest, but does he have the emotional maturity to handle the ups and downs of a romance?

Take it from me, a child psychologist with two decades of experience, a child of nine to twelve is too young for romantic relationships. Empathize with your child's feelings, but there can be a lot of heartache that comes with romantic relationships, and children of that age usually aren't equipped with the emotional savvy to deal with it. It will be virtually impossible to prevent your child from starting a romance if that is what he

has decided he wants to do. Here are some ways you can express your concern and, hopefully, open up a critical and ongoing dialogue with your child on this subject:

- "You've got lots of time to be a grown-up and do grown-up activities like dating, but you don't have much time left to be a kid. I would like you to slow things down. What do you think about that?"

- "Romantic relationships take a lot of time and energy. They can be a lot of work! It's okay to change your mind if you realize you don't want to have a boyfriend yet. I'm here to listen if you want to talk about it."

- "I don't feel comfortable with the idea of you dating just yet. I need you to know that, but I also want you to know that you can talk to me about anything—even if you've started having a relationship."

- "I don't think you're ready to be dating. If you have made that choice, I hope you have done some thinking about boundaries—how you will treat that person and also how you will allow yourself to be treated. I'm here if you have any questions or worries."

Kids have a lot of time before they need to worry about romance. Encourage them not to rush it.

MORE FROM TYLER'S STORY

As we consider bullying and early romances, let's revisit Tyler, who we met in chapter 5. You'll recall him as the middle schooler who was tricked by a group of classmates into sexting with an online "girlfriend" (via a fake social media account); eventually, these classmates embarrassed him by soliciting and distributing a naked photo of him. (Note that these kids faced legal ramifications for their actions.)

It's obvious that these kids weren't the right friends for Tyler. In counseling sessions, he and I talked a lot about what makes a good friend and what doesn't. We discussed what matters more, being cool or having a few solid friends who have your back. Tyler's family participated in the sessions as well. He was able to identify a couple of good friends in his life but those friends didn't live close by, and he wasn't able to see them without planning and rides from his parents. In session, his parents were able to commit to doing whatever it took to facilitate these better friendships.

Tyler decided not to switch schools because that naked picture had made the rounds at all the nearby schools; we decided together that it was better for him to hold his head up high and return to his school, despite the challenges. His parents did a good job of helping him to destigmatize his situation. His boundaries had been violated and kids at school and elsewhere had seen his body. That was embarrassing, but everyone has a body and there's nothing shameful about sexuality. With the help of his family and his good friends, Tyler was able to move forward.

Tyler's father, in particular, was helpful in nurturing good friendships and creating bonding moments. In one great example, Tyler's dad purchased three season-pass tickets to a local team, and regularly took Tyler and a friend to baseball games. This gave Tyler an easy, fun way to reach out to other kids and begin to create healthier friendships at his school, and his dad had an opportunity to support, observe, and assist in this process.

***

Prioritizing healthy, real-life human connection is going to become increasingly important as our children's generation progresses to adulthood in a screen-addicted world. Emphasizing the value and importance of human connections while your children are young will position them to cherish real-life relationships into their teens and adulthood.

By the time they hit the tween years, kids are choosing their own friends and deciding which activities they'll participate in. That is part of the reason why middle school is so hard for some kids. If your child feels confident about her peer group and ability to relate to classmates and/or team-mates, she will be better able to navigate the rough waters of adolescence.

Your child's self-confidence will augment the relationship you as a parent are developing with her, and eventually, when your child becomes a teenager, you'll be able to talk naturally with her about the fact that abstaining from sex doesn't mean abstaining from intimacy. As your child ages, understanding the distinction between sex and intimacy will become more important, and you need to be able to discuss these things with her without either of you feeling that the subject is taboo.

Yeah...I guess he didn't feel very good.

I imagine he almost felt invisible, like he didn't even exist in their eyes.

I never really thought about it like that. Why do some people live on the street?

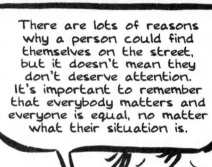

There are lots of reasons why a person could find themselves on the street, but it doesn't mean they don't deserve attention. It's important to remember that everybody matters and everyone is equal, no matter what their situation is.

Okay Mom.

Maybe there's something we can do to help!

What three activities or events can you facilitate in the coming month to help your child nurture meaningful relationships? How can you help them maintain these relationships?

_____

_____

_____

_____

_____

_____

_____

_____

_____

_____

_____

_____

_____

_____

_____

_____

_____

_____

_____

_____

_____

_____

_____

_____

CHAPTER 7

LOSE STIGMA AND PREJUDICE

Over many generations, our society has turned anything having to do with sex into a taboo subject, unsuitable for discussion in polite company, much less with children. Talking about sex is just not something most people do on a regular basis. Whether the topic is sex itself, sex education for our children, our own sexuality, or the sexual identity of our friends and neighbors, there is a sense of shock when a person talks openly about it, and often a sense of shame as well. We must let that go.

As I said earlier, we as parents do not have the luxury of being squeamish about sex. Denial or silence will harm our children, given what they are exposed to in our hypersexualized world. Sex is natural, and it must be discussed naturally. It's paradoxical that the subject of sex remains taboo in a world that has become saturated with both innuendo and overtly explicit sexual content. Perhaps this very stigma around sex is what has driven much of mass culture toward graphic, hollow, and unrealistic portrayals of what real sexual intimacy is. If the

subject were discussed more honestly and openly in the home, I wonder whether fewer young people would find themselves "driven underground" by their unanswered questions?

To develop a healthy understanding of relationships, a child must first have a healthy understanding of his own self. Talks about sex can—and should—be had in an age-appropriate yet straightforward manner. When we become more comfortable talking about sex, we have to also become more comfortable talking about stigma, because they are so often related. In the context of sexuality, I offer two ways to accomplish this:

1. Talk openly about sex and topics related to sexuality.

2. Reject prejudice against and hate for those who have a different sexual orientation and/or gender identity.

Children need to be taught to embrace diversity early in their lives, and you can do this by actively modeling an attitude of openness in your home.

It is time for parents to lose any prejudices when it comes to gender or sexual orientation. This means not hiding the issue when a friend or family member is LGBTQ+ (lesbian, gay, bisexual, transgender, queer or questioning, plus other evolving identities) or different in any way. The world is full of people with different thoughts, feelings, and preferences, and these differences mean that people, and relationships, come in a variety of shapes and sizes—all of which are beautiful. By demonstrating your openness, respect, and acceptance of diversity, you can help your child if he (or she) struggles with his identity or has a friend who is questioning. You can model supportive behavior when you speak with friends or family members.

Developing a Sexual Identity

Sexual identity is best understood as a spectrum, and coming to understand our identity is a fluid process that evolves over time as we reach mature adulthood. It can even change after that. As your child moves from childhood toward adolescence, she (or he) may begin to explore her identity, or you may privately wonder if she is going to present as straight, gay, or something else. Give your child the freedom to explore what it means to be her authentic self. It is vital that you provide unconditional love and acceptance at this juncture.

Sexual identity is unique to each individual and is central to the person's core. Even in a child who is not sexually active, core identity can be tied to gender or future sexuality and may be traditional or nontraditional. There is *nothing* more important you can do as a parent than supporting your child through struggles with her identity.

Sexual development begins at birth, according to *Sexual Development and Behavior in Children—Information for Parents & Caregivers*, a downloadable resource put out by the National Child Traumatic Stress Network in partnership with the National Center on Sexual Behavior of Youth, available on their website, www. nctsn. org. Sexual development includes not only the physical changes that occur as children grow, but also the sexual knowledge and beliefs they come to learn and the behaviors they show.

Here are additional key concepts shared by those organizations:

- When children are in grade school (approximately ages seven to twelve), their awareness of social rules increases and they become more modest and want more privacy, particularly around adults. Although self-touch (masturbation) and sexual play continue, children at this age are likely to hide these activities from adults.
- Curiosity about adult sexual behavior increases—particularly as puberty approaches—and children

may begin to seek out sexual content in television, movies, and printed material. Telling jokes and "dirty" stories is common. Children approaching puberty are likely to start displaying romantic and sexual interest in their peers.

Although parents often become concerned when a child shows sexual behavior, such as touching another child's private parts, these behaviors are not uncommon in developing children. Most sexual play is an expression of children's natural curiosity and should not be a cause for concern or alarm. Though this behavior is not cause for punishment or a harsh reaction on your part, this would be a good time to reinforce the concept of boundaries and explain to your child that it is natural to be curious but it is inappropriate to touch the private parts of others, and other children should not be touching theirs. If you come across your child participating in touching with another child, it may be a good idea to inform the other child's parents. If the parents of the other child are upset, acknowledge that the behavior was not appropriate and explain that you are having/will have ongoing conversations about boundaries with your child—hopefully, they will do the same.

Often when children participate in sexual behavior, they are indicating that they need to learn something. Teach the child what she needs to

know, given the situation. For example, your child may be curious about what the body of the opposite gender looks like or if her body looks similar to another child of the same gender. So your child may benefit from looking at a book about the human body.

At around age ten, children make a leap in their cognition potential and go from seeing things in a very concrete way to being able to handle more abstract thought. Most children tend to identify with others of the same gender early on, and as they get older, they become more and more attracted to the opposite gender. There are children who are gender fluid, meaning they do not identify with any fixed gender; there are also those who may always identify with the other gender; and there are children who may be attracted to members of their own gender.

Parents, don't assume that your child is straight or gay. Stereotypes of characteristics are just that, a simplistic way of categorizing people. A child who is questioning their identity is going through a process that can be extremely confusing. Show your child that you are nonjudgmental and will help them along their journey of self-discovery. You can show this by being open to talking with them about their exploration. Educate yourself and your family about LGBTQ+ issues. Watch movies that explore this topic. Talk with others who may have gone through a similar questioning process.

One of the ways you can show respect for others' identities—and, possibly, your child's—is by using the pronouns that the person chooses. A person may choose a pronoun that does not conform to the gender assigned at birth, or may prefer a gender-neutral pronoun. It is becoming more common to ask people which pronouns they use, and using a person's preferred pronouns is a sign of respect for the person's gender identity.

As you may have noticed, throughout much of this book I have used "he/him/his" and "she/her/hers" randomly to refer to generic individuals, and sometimes I use "they/them/their"; this is because the English language does not have a gender-neutral singular pronoun. Some people are choosing new gender-neutral pronouns such as "zie/zim/zir" or others to refer to themselves. Using "they" to refer to an individual is becoming far more common in casual usage, and increasingly common in formal usage. Because we talk in this chapter about people who may be questioning the way they identify or who may prefer a gender-neutral pronoun, you'll see that I use "they/them/their" more often.

Participate in activities that make your child feel accepted and part of a community of others who are like them. But don't push. If your child isn't sure how they are feeling and what identity feels authentic, let them work through it. There's no need for a definitive answer at this point in their lives; they need time to sort through their feelings and grow into themselves. Just be there to offer love and support.

The Power of Self-Esteem

When children understand what makes them unique in a positive way, they begin to get a better sense of self. What comes along with that is the confidence to *be* themselves. The most powerful factor for equipping kids to handle the increasingly complex, sexualized world they are entering is self-esteem.

A child who not only feels good about herself but believes in her own abilities and future success has a protective barrier. The child with a strong concept of self won't feel as great a need to prove anything to anyone, to change herself, or to please others by crossing boundaries. This is key because finding acceptance in a peer group is a top concern of tweens and teens. Children who feel desperate to find or create a sense of belonging are at risk of engaging in unhealthy behaviors. In contrast, children with a strong sense of self are likely to be more intrinsically than extrinsically motivated, meaning that they seek validation from within themselves rather than looking for feedback from peers. Negative outside influences don't hold as much power.

Model Healthy Attitudes

As parents, we need to be mindful of what we say and do. Unless there is a specific situation that prompts you to sit down and talk directly with your preteen about homosexuality, you may not choose to do so, but you can certainly be careful to model healthy, inclusive attitudes. By demonstrating your openness, respect, and acceptance of diversity, you can help your child if/when he has a friend who is struggling with identity. You can model supportive behavior when you speak with neighbors or other families who may be going through their own struggles. Following are some ways to do that.

THINK ABOUT YOUR PUT-DOWNS

It may not have occurred to you to think about your word choices when you put someone down, but there's power in words. Sometimes our comments come out of our mouths so fast, filled with expressions we may have used for years, that we hardly consider what we are saying. As a psychologist, I might wish that no one ever used derogatory terms, but I know that's not the reality. So I challenge you to think about the words and phrases you use. Some people use homosexuality-based words such as, "That's gay" or "You're a homo." Others may use gender-based words such as, "He's crying like a little girl" or "Her hair is so short she looks like a boy." Be aware of your language,

and do your best to strip your conversation of words and phrases that diminish marginalized groups.

REALIZE IT'S NOT A JOKING MATTER

If you defend a person from an inappropriate joke targeted at their sexuality, that act will leave an impression on your child, and may even change your own mindset. When someone stands up for another, a kinship develops, even if the two people don't know each other or have any other interactions. Here are some responses you might think about using when you hear an offensive joke.

- "You may not realize how rude/disrespectful that joke is, let's talk about something else."

- "Jokes about people's sexuality aren't funny."

- "I don't think it's funny to mock people who are different."

HAVE ZERO TOLERANCE FOR HATE

Parents can insist that others in their home abide by their rules. Having a zero-tolerance policy for hateful or discriminatory language from your children, their friends, and other adults demonstrates by example your expectation that everyone be treated fairly and with respect. You don't have to be confrontational when outlining your rules; you can simply model appropriate responses, such as, "We don't use words like _____ in our house" or "All people are worthy of respect, and what you said is not respectful." Your child will then know how to respond when she hears such talk from others.

UNDERSCORE THAT SEXUALITY IS NOT IDENTITY

It's great to have people who are different in your family or community, but they need to be celebrated for who they are, not what they are. It's important not to hide someone's sexuality and to talk with your children about what that means, but it's equally important that you don't make that the one thing you talk about all the time. People who are LGBTQ+ don't need their sexuality referenced every time you talk about them. Find something else as a reference point. For example, instead of "Cousin Patti, you remember her, the one who's a lesbian?" you could say something like, "Cousin Patti, remember . . . the one who came over last Christmas and beat all of us at Monopoly?"

LOOK BEYOND BLUE AND PINK

There are no gender differences in toys or clothing, only societal stereotypes. Allow your kids to wear or play with whatever they want to, and don't make a big deal about a boy wanting to play dress-up or a girl choosing to zoom around the sandbox with a tractor. Every child deserves to make these benign choices according to their own preferences, and a choice today on a shirt or a doll doesn't portend

anything for the future. Children who dress the way they want, whether in a mismatched outfit or a color associated with the other gender, and do the things they like to do will feel good about themselves—and that's what we want to instill in our children: confidence and self-esteem.

SHOW SUPPORT

When you and your family participate in events that show support for families in your community, especially families that aren't like yours, you are modeling empathy, inclusiveness, and community service. Helping your child see that you care about issues even when they might not affect you personally sets the stage for your child's future engagement in the community. Activities such as taking your family to a Pride event, volunteering at a hospital for sick children, and making hygiene packets to hand out to homeless people all show your child that the health and well-being of an entire community are the responsibility of all the members of that community.

CHOOSE DIVERSE MEDIA

Children grow up with inclusive mindsets when they are exposed to diversity from a young age. It is much easier to form fundamentally accepting values from early childhood than it is to reverse or change misinformed values later in life. Exposing kids to a range of toys, books, and TV shows that represent diversity of gender, race, religion, and sexual identity teaches your child that the world is an interesting place full of different kinds of people—all of whom have value and unique contributions.

Support for LGBTQ+ Youth

Identity and orientation aren't binary classifications—you're either this or that. Today, gender is best understood as a continuum. At various stages of development, children may identify more with one end of the gender spectrum or the other, just as some will be attracted to one gender more than the other. This is normal, and where they are on one day doesn't mean that's where they'll be on another day. The same goes for sexuality. Some people find that they are more attracted to the opposite gender, others will feel attracted to the same. Parents should know that gender and sexuality are much more complex and nuanced than we realized previously. If you've always believed gender and sexual orientation are rigid and set at birth, this different way of thinking can be difficult to wrap your head around.

In an effort to educate, here is a quick list of identifications, from the Egale Canada Human Rights Trust, that are commonly experienced today:

bisexual (adj or n): A person who is attracted emotionally and sexually to both male-identified and female-identified people.

cisgender (adj): A person who identifies with the gender associated with their birth-assigned sex. Someone who is cisgender may identify as straight, gay, and so on.

gay (adj or n): A person who is emotionally and sexually attracted to someone of the same sex and/or gender—gay can include both male-identified individuals and female-identified individuals, or refer to male-identified individuals only.

gender identity (n): A person's deeply felt internal and individual experience of gender—their internal sense of being a man, woman, or another gender entirely. A person's gender may or may not correspond with the sex assigned to them at birth. Because gender identity is internal, one's gender identity is not necessarily visible to others.

lesbian (adj or n): A female-identified person who is emotionally and sexually attracted to female-identified people.

LGBTQ+: An acronym for "lesbian, gay, bisexual, transgender, transsexual, two-spirit, queer and questioning" people.

queer (adj or n or v): Historically, a derogatory term for homosexuality, used to insult LGBT people. Although still used as a slur by some, the term has been reclaimed by some members of LGBT communities, particularly youth. In its reclaimed form it can be used as a symbol of pride and affirmation of difference and diversity, or as a means of challenging rigid identity categories.

questioning (adj or n or v): A person who is unsure of their sexual orientation or gender identity.

sexual orientation (n): A person's capacity for profound emotional and sexual attraction to another person based on their sex and/or gender.

trans (adj): A term commonly used to refer to transgender, transsexual, and/or gender variant identities and experiences. Although it is often used as an umbrella term, some people identify just as trans.

transgender (adj or n): A person who does not identify either fully or in part with the gender associated with their birth-assigned sex—often used as an umbrella term to represent a wide range of gender identities and expressions. Transgender people (just like cisgender people) may identify as straight, gay, and so on.

transsexual (adj or n): A person whose sex assigned at birth does not correspond with their gender identity. A transsexual woman needs to live and experience life as a woman and a transsexual man needs to live and experience life as a man. Many identify as transgender, rather than transsexual, because they are uncomfortable with the psychiatric connections to the term "transsexual." Some transsexual people may physically alter their body (e.g., sex reassignment surgery and/or hormone therapy) and gender expression to correspond with their gender identity.

two spirit (or two-spirit or 2-spirit) (adj): Some aboriginal people choose to identify as two spirit rather than, or in addition to, identifying as lesbian, gay, bisexual, trans, or queer. Prior to European colonization, two-spirit people were respected members of their communities and were often accorded special status based upon their unique abilities to understand both male and female perspectives. Two-spirit persons were often the visionaries, healers, and medicine people in their communities. The term "two spirit" affirms the interrelatedness of all aspects of identity—including gender, sexuality, community, culture, and spirituality. It is an English term used to stand in for the many aboriginal language words for two spirit.

It's important for parents to communicate unconditional love to their children, and to stress that their love is not in any way based on the child's gender or sexuality but on their whole being. Parents, if your children—or your children's friends—are questioning their gender or their sexual identity, educate yourselves, talk with a trusted friend or professional, and try to understand the self-discovery process your child is going through in order to identify their authentic self. You may find that your process of understanding can take a lot of time, patience, and openness, and it may be helpful to reach out to a local counselor or find specific resources in your area to help you on this journey.

You also need to know that LGBTQ+ youth are at an increased risk of abuse and harassment as well as homelessness, mental illness, and suicide—and many of these risks stem from problems or rejection at home. One 2009 study of Boston high schoolers found that LGBTQ youth showed more symptoms of depression and were many times more likely to report self-harm and suicidal ideation than their heterosexual, cisgender classmates. Another study of transgender persons in San Francisco found that 32 percent had attempted suicide and concluded that suicide prevention interventions for transgender persons were "urgently needed, particularly for young people."

Acceptance from family members and the child's school community are of the greatest importance when it comes to a child who is LGBTQ+. Lesbian, gay, bisexual, transsexual, transgender, and queer youth are overrepresented in the homeless youth population in North America, according to a survey from 2014. Supportive environments *do* make a huge difference in their lives and well-being. In fact, a 2011 study in Oregon found the risk of attempting suicide for lesbian, gay, or bisexual youth was 20 percent *greater* in social environments unsupportive of LGBTQ persons compared with in supportive environments.

So it is critical that any child questioning their sexual identity have the support of their parents, schools, and community, no matter the circumstances. By demonstrating your openness, respect, and acceptance of diversity, you can help your child or another student in the community. That support is contagious, so if one child feels it, and more kids know how to offer support, then others will start to feel it, too. Even one act of kindness and understanding can have a ripple effect.

If you or your spouse are struggling to accept your child's identity, consider going to counseling together. The matter needs to be addressed because any kind of prejudice inside the family can harm your child. No child should ever feel unloved by their parents or feel shame or a lack of belonging in their family. The need to feel accepted is a basic need that is best met by the people closest to the child.

Drew's Story

Drew's troubled coming-out story is unfortunately too common in our society. In high school, Drew came out as gay to his sister and his mom, but was concerned about his father's reaction. His mom, while supportive of him as a person, worried about his safety in their rather conservative community and told her son, "Don't breathe a word to anyone. You're going to be eaten alive if you do." Mom was clearly speaking from a knee-jerk reaction to her own fears, but what message did her son receive? That his mom wanted him to deny the real feelings he was experiencing. Mom could have said, "Okay, thank you for telling me this. I'm not sure now is a good time to talk about that with your dad or at school, but why don't we make you an appointment to talk it through with someone who understands these issues?"

Instead Drew thought about ways he might "soften the blow" to his dad and his friends. He tentatively mentioned being attracted to both girls and boys, but rather than introducing the idea that he was gay, Drew's ambiguity allowed his dad to brush off his explanations. Dad dismissed Drew's attraction to boys as a phase, telling him to "focus on girls" and confirming Drew's worst fears.

Eventually Drew's mom understood that he couldn't deny his true self, and for a while Drew went about his life with the support of his mother and sister. Later, he began a relationship with a boy at school. At first, this boy was introduced as simply a friend. When Drew's dad learned that they were more than friends, he exploded. The revelation occurred at a family birthday party and caused a heated

argument. Word spread through their small community and exacerbated the problem. Time didn't heal these wounds, and the family dynamic grew increasingly toxic over the following weeks and months, with no reconciliation of dad to Drew's identity as gay. He also faced incessant bullying from peers. The ramifications for Drew and every member of his family were long-lasting.

The moral of the story is that parents need to look beyond their concerns of stigma or their own prejudice when a child is working through issues of their sexuality or identity. Failing to do so puts the family, as well as the mental health of the child, at risk. Parents need to focus on the person their child is becoming, giving them space in certain areas if that's what they need. Refusing to accept a child for who they are can cost not just the relationship with the child, but the relationship with the entire family. Parents who are struggling with their feelings about lifestyle or sexual orientation must carefully consider the implications for their children if they cannot overcome those feelings and create conditions of love and safety for their children as they grow into their own.

***

Sexuality, in and of itself, is a challenging topic, and it's important to be comfortable—or to get comfortable fast—with this subject matter. That's not easy for some, but it will pay off in the long run. Whether or not your family includes a child who struggles with their sexuality or identity, it's important to provide unconditional love and lose any stigma or prejudice. As you will see in the next chapter, as long as a groundwork of protective factors has been established, kids and families are able to face challenges and move through difficult periods with minimal collateral damage or lasting effects.

It's never easy to learn that a child you love may be on a more challenging path, but I congratulate you for doing the hard work to move past stigma and prejudice. You will need to follow up on that hard work by building up that child's self-esteem and resilience, both of which can be worn like a protective suit of armor.

Mom, kids at school are saying things about Evan! They say that Evan has a boyfriend, that he's gay!

It sounds like they're talking about being gay as a bad thing. That's not right. There's nothing wrong with being attracted to somebody else, no matter who that is.

Your brother is exploring his feelings, and that's normal. This is the time of his life when he's supposed to figure things out.

I thought boys were supposed to like girls, and girls were supposed to like boys.

Well, that might be what you see a lot of times, but it's not how things always work. Sometimes boys like boys and girls like girls.

Sometimes people like both girls and boys. It doesn't matter! What is important is that Evan is finding out who he is and, as his family, we're going to support him.

I'm afraid what Dad is going to say. I'm afraid what Grandma and Grandpa will say!

We all love Evan and that will never change. And even if one person doesn't understand, it won't matter because Dad and I will be here to help Evan and support him in all the ways that we can.

We would do the same for you!

Take a moment to think about any shame, stigma, or prejudice you may have. How can you take steps to work through it to ensure your child does not carry the same burden?

_____

_____

_____

_____

_____

_____

_____

_____

_____

_____

_____

_____

_____

_____

_____

_____

_____

_____

_____

_____

_____

_____

_____

CHAPTER 8

BUILD RESILIENCE

The previous points of the Parental Compass—Start Early, Give Unconditional Love, Stay Current, Set Smart Boundaries, Nurture Relationships, and Lose Stigma and Prejudice—all converge here, where we talk about building your child's resilience. Given that today's parents encounter situations with their children that they never faced growing up, we know that questions and dilemmas will emerge. The best way to strengthen our children is by constantly helping them to develop resilience, so that when they confront a difficult situation, both the child and the family can bounce back from it more easily.

You may be asking yourself, what exactly is resilience? My definition of resilience is this: It's the ability of a person to navigate through a challenging experience—a trauma or a set of difficult circumstances—and get to the other side successfully. Although the definition of difficult circumstances may be different for each person, everyone has the inherent capacity to become resilient.

Poverty, bullying, or a car accident are examples of challenges a person may face, and in each case, resilience can make a difference in the way that person overcomes the challenge. To some, a bad grade in school is a big hurdle, while for others the crisis may be a cancer diagnosis. Circumstances can vary greatly, as can the level of resilience needed to get through them. Every parent can and should nurture resilience in their children, because at some point in their lives, they will face something difficult.

Resilience involves behaviors and mindsets that anyone can develop. It is different from self-confidence (trusting in oneself and one's ability to engage with the world), but it is no less powerful. Fostering resilience is akin to vaccinating your child—you are inoculating the child against harmful forces, both internal and external.

Risk, Resilience, and Recovery

Earlier, I likened resilience to a Teflon coating for your child. It's about hope, and practicing strategies to build resilience boosts your child's odds of recovering from adversity. All of the points on the Parental Compass work together, complement one another, and bring us to this final point, the goal of the entire book: building your child's resilience.

Every child will encounter risk factors at some point in her life. Facing the world with eyes wide open, we can equip our kids with the tools they need to navigate hazards—and they'll carry those tools with them into adulthood. We know we cannot be there for every moment, and we certainly can't prevent every bad thing from happening. Sheltering your child from the realities of life won't do her any favors, and the best way to prepare her is to build up her resilience before she ever needs it.

Some common risk factors that children might face are stress, anxiety, bullying, change in primary peer circle, poverty, lack of unconditional love from a parent or caregiver, social isolation, academic troubles, high conflict in the home, divorce, illness/disability, exposure to inappropriate sexual material and, in extreme situations, addiction/substance abuse and abuse/neglect. Building resilience in children who experience these problems is much harder, but a caring adult can help a child overcome even these most difficult of challenges.

LOOKING AT THE RESEARCH
In 1955, a group of child health professionals (doctors, psychologists, social workers, and others) began a prospective study of nearly seven hundred babies born that year on the Hawaiian island of Kauai. The purpose of the study was to track the children's development into adulthood and record key outcomes pertaining to vulnerability and resilience. The researchers followed these babies for more than three decades.

Risk, Resilience, and Recovery: Perspectives from the Kauai Longitudinal Study, published by Emmy E. Werner, Ph.D., of the University of California, Davis, in 1993, chronicled that long-term study. I have found plenty of evidence in my clinical psychology practice to support Werner's research and theory that many children are able to make positive adaptations and surmount even the most challenging circumstances.

Of particular interest were those identified as "high risk"—about 30 percent of the children in the study. Researchers noticed that among this high-risk group (criteria included families in poverty, parents with addiction, subjection to early trauma), about one in three of the kids grew into well-adjusted, self-actualized adults. They were as accomplished as the low-risk group from stable, affluent upbringings, while the other two-thirds in the high-risk group grew up to face developmental/behavioral challenges, mental illness, delinquency, teen pregnancy, criminality, and other negative outcomes. All the children in the high-risk group were subjected to more or less equal risk factors, so why did some emerge into adulthood successfully, while others did not?

The difference, Werner discovered, lay in a matrix of protective factors, conditions that were more prevalent in the lives of the successful group than in the other group. These protective factors included:

- Positive temperament

- Good social group

- At least one consistent and unconditionally supportive person who is not the child's parent

- Extracurricular participation

- Being the oldest in the family (because of responsibility)

- Academic success

- A spiritual life

- Guidance during times of transition, i.e., access to good information

The fascinating—and hopeful—takeaway from this study is that children can build protective factors, which mitigate against vulnerabilities. These protective factors can even level the playing field for children who face multiple challenges not of their own making, such as poverty or trauma. Kids *can* bounce back. This is good news for parents who are looking at the troubling landscape ahead and wondering whether their child will be able to make it through. The answer is yes! I'll show you how to help your child cultivate the protective factors that will help him surmount any obstacles he faces in life.

DEVELOPMENTAL ASSETS

Werner's work was the foundational research that inspired many others to study human resilience more extensively. The Search Institute of Minneapolis has led the way in creating a concise summary of the most important developmental assets, also called protective factors, organized by age group. I routinely refer to this group's Top 40 Developmental Assets in my clinical work and also in my teaching. These are the building blocks that help young people grow up healthy, caring, and responsible. The lists include external assets and internal assets, all of which a child can develop:

External Assets

- **Support:** To be surrounded by people who love, care for, appreciate, and accept them.

- **Empowerment:** To feel valued and valuable. This happens when kids feel safe and respected.

- **Boundaries and expectations:** Clear rules, consistent consequences for breaking rules, and encouragement to do their best.

- **Constructive use of time:** Opportunities—outside of school—to learn and develop new skills and interests with other youths and adults.

Internal Assets

- **Commitment to learning:** A sense of the lasting importance of learning and a belief in their own abilities.

- **Positive values:** Strong guiding values or principles to help them make healthy life choices.

- **Social competencies:** The skills to interact effectively with others, to make difficult decisions, and to cope with new situations.

- **Positive identity:** Belief in their own self-worth and a feeling that they have control over the things that happen to them.

I routinely share these lists with parents so they're aware of the steps they can take to mitigate the risk factors that may exist in their child's life. Parents often feel validated after reading the list, as they recognize the things they are already doing. They also find the lists useful for getting new ideas and additional ways they can support their children's resilience.

Children can also learn "positive temperament," which is a primary protective factor. This may be something a person is born with, but it can also be nurtured in the home by parents. A positive temperament allows a person to take a negative experience and pivot quickly to another, more positive, activity. Parents can model this

behavior for their children, showing them a way to keep moving forward amid adversity. A positive temperament can be an attitude choice.

Opportunities for Building Resilience

The best way to build your child's resilience is by giving him a sense of purpose beyond himself. Show your child that he can be a change agent and apply his energy to making the world a better place! This will have the added benefit of broadening his worldview. The following are some suggestions from my FamilySparks.com Global Citizenship Course, which promotes resilience building.

OFFER MEANINGFUL CHOICES

From a young age, involve your children in decision making. This can start with simple choices during the preschool years, such as, "Which sweater would you like to wear?" or "Do you want to draw a picture or bake cookies?" As your child grows, increase the significance of his choices. Some options for inviting input include:

- Where to go for a family trip

- What to name a new pet

- Which projects to do around the house or yard

- How to commemorate special events or milestones

40 DEVELOPMENTAL ASSETS® FOR MIDDLE CHILDHOOD (AGES 8–12)

Search Institute® has identified the following building blocks of healthy development—known as Developmental Assets®—that help young people grow up healthy, caring, and responsible.

EXTERNAL ASSETS

Support	1. **Family support**—Family life provides high levels of love and support.
	2. **Positive family communication**—Parent(s) and child communicate positively. Child feels comfortable seeking advice and counsel from parent(s).
	3. **Other adult relationships**—Child receives support from adults other than her or his parent(s).
	4. **Caring neighborhood**—Child experiences caring neighbors.
	5. **Caring school climate**—Relationships with teachers and peers provide a caring, encouraging environment.
	6. **Parent involvement in schooling**—Parent(s) are actively involved in helping the child succeed in school.
Empowerment	7. **Community values youth**—Child feels valued and appreciated by adults in the community.
	8. **Children as resources**—Child is included in decisions at home and in the community.
	9. **Service to others**—Child has opportunities to help others in the community.
	10. **Safety**—Child feels safe at home, at school, and in his or her neighborhood.
Boundaries & Expectations	11. **Family boundaries**—Family has clear and consistent rules and consequences and monitors the child's whereabouts.
	12. **School Boundaries**—School provides clear rules and consequences.
	13. **Neighborhood boundaries**—Neighbors take responsibility for monitoring the child's behavior.
	14. **Adult role models**—Parent(s) and other adults in the child's family, as well as nonfamily adults, model positive, responsible behavior.
	15. **Positive peer influence**—Child's closest friends model positive, responsible behavior.
	16. **High expectations**—Parent(s) and teachers expect the child to do her or his best at school and in other activities.
Constructive Use of Time	17. **Creative activities**—Child participates in music, art, drama, or creative writing two or more times per week.
	18. **Child programs**—Child participates two or more times per week in cocurricular school activities or structured community programs for children.
	19. **Religious community**—Child attends religious programs or services one or more times per week.
	20. **Time at home**—Child spends some time most days both in high-quality interaction with parents and doing things at home other than watching TV or playing video games.

(continued on next page)

INTERNAL ASSETS	**Commitment to Learning**	21. **Achievement Motivation**—Child is motivated and strives to do well in school. 22. **Learning Engagement**—Child is responsive, attentive, and actively engaged in learning at school and enjoys participating in learning activities outside of school. 23. **Homework**—Child usually hands in homework on time. 24. **Bonding to school**—Child cares about teachers and other adults at school. 25. **Reading for Pleasure**—Child enjoys and engages in reading for fun most days of the week.
	Positive Values	26. **Caring**—Parent(s) tell the child it is important to help other people. 27. **Equality and social justice**—Parent(s) tell the child it is important to speak up for equal rights for all people. 28. **Integrity**—Parent(s) tell the child it is important to stand up for one's beliefs. 29. **Honesty**—Parent(s) tell the child it is important to tell the truth. 30. **Responsibility**—Parent(s) tell the child it is important to accept personal responsibility for behavior. 31. **Healthy Lifestyle**—Parent(s) tell the child it is important to have good health habits and an understanding of healthy sexuality.
	Social Competencies	32. **Planning and decision making**—Child thinks about decisions and is usually happy with results of her or his decisions. 33. **Interpersonal Competence**—Child cares about and is affected by other people's feelings, enjoys making friends, and, when frustrated or angry, tries to calm her- or himself. 34. **Cultural Competence**—Child knows and is comfortable with people of different racial, ethnic, and cultural backgrounds and with her or his own cultural identity. 35. **Resistance skills**—Child can stay away from people who are likely to get her or him in trouble and is able to say no to doing wrong or dangerous things. 36. **Peaceful conflict resolution**—Child seeks to resolve conflict nonviolently.
	Positive Identity	37. **Personal power**—Child feels he or she has some influence over things that happen in her or his life. 38. **Self-esteem**—Child likes and is proud to be the person that he or she is. 39. **Sense of purpose**—Child sometimes thinks about what life means and whether there is a purpose for her or his life. 40. **Positive view of personal future**—Child is optimistic about her or his personal future

Including your children in decision making, when appropriate, helps cultivate their sense of agency as they grow older. It also gives them the opportunity for leadership, and you should look for more ways to let them spearhead a project from start to finish. The outcome—good, bad, or in between—will also offer a valuable lesson.

LET KIDS PROBLEM SOLVE

When something is wrong, parents may automatically jump into "solution mode" and solve children's problems for them. We do this because we love them and don't want to see them struggle, and because as adults we have developed advanced problem-solving skills. Children can also develop excellent problem-solving skills, *if given opportunities to practice*. The sooner your child learns this mindset, the better able he will be to react to dilemmas when you are not around.

If there is a problem at school or home or in a friendship, ask your child whether he has any ideas for solutions before supplying answers. Of course, you will need to provide guidance and support if he is struggling with a solution, but see what he comes up with first and then talk through the idea with him.

LET YOUR CHILD HAVE A VOICE, THEN LISTEN!

In many situations we prepare our kids to speak out but we don't prepare adults to listen to the unique wisdom kids possess. Take the time to listen carefully to your child and consider her point of view. When possible, gently encourage other adults to do the same.

Giving your child the floor during discussions allows her to share her thoughts and boosts her confidence, but also introduces a new perspective into the conversation. It can be quite amazing to discover the ideas and solutions that live inside a child's mind. Pay attention—it might just be the best idea in the room.

ALLOW KIDS TO SET THEIR OWN TERMS

Kids need ways to participate meaningfully in our society and have responsibilities that are proportionate to their stage of development. You can play a role by facilitating opportunities for your child to get involved in activities, organizations, and events. If your child has an interest that isn't supported at school, encourage him to create his own opportunity. Ask permission to start an afterschool club. Maybe your child has noticed litter on the beach or in a park, so you could suggest that he form a cleanup crew with other kids from the neighborhood.

The next time you plan a family party or function, ask your child for input and give him a meaningful role, such as assisting with food prep, planning the menu, setting up the house, or making invitations. Then let him do his job and resist the urge to micromanage. Opportunities like these will give your child the self-confidence to roll up his sleeves and participate in his broader community. Supporting your child as he develops a sense of responsibility and leadership skills is a critical protective factor.

IDENTIFY YOUR FAMILY VALUES

Having well-defined family values gives your children a strong foundation and reference point from which to govern their own behavior and choices as they grow up. I believe children should have input in shaping family values, as it makes them active participants in the process, rendering those values more meaningful.

Take note of what your child cares about and see how that can be connected to one of your family's values. For example, if your child cares deeply about animal rights, you might commit to buying only humanely raised meat or going vegetarian a few days a week. Or if one of your family values is giving back to your community, you could create a tradition of volunteering as a family at a soup kitchen every month.

ENGAGE AS A FAMILY

Volunteering or serving together as a family is a meaningful experience with many positive benefits for children. The most obvious is learning the importance of service to others, but the added bonus is that your family is spending time together, which strengthens your bond. You have an opportunity to model service behavior for your kids and participate in service learning. This will create memories together that your children will carry with them into adulthood.

Here are a few of the core benefits your child can experience through volunteering as a family:

- A sense of responsibility: Learning responsibility from a young age promotes accountability. It also fosters a positive growth mindset that allows a child to use an obstacle as an opportunity to learn and progress.

- The virtue of tolerance, which will serve your child well as he progresses toward adulthood in an increasingly diverse and connected world.

- The idea that one person can make a difference in the world. Seeing the effect of one's actions helps to build self-confidence and support intrinsic motivation, which comes from internal values and isn't influenced by outside factors.

- Your child will learn valuable skills that will prepare her for future responsibilities, such as a job, when she gets older.

More from Emily's Story

To give you an idea of the power of resilience, I want to return to Emily, the fourteen-year-old girl we met in chapter 4. Emily desperately wanted to fit in when she started high school, and thought she had to do that through sexual behavior. She equated popularity with sexual activity, and some of the boys in her school took full advantage. Emily could have had long-term problems, but her parents and I pulled in the points of the Parental Compass to help her heal.

GIVE UNCONDITIONAL LOVE

Emily's parents displayed the unconditional love they have for her throughout her troubled situation. They were completely present for her and wanted to hear about her life and what was important. Mom and dad took turns having weekly lunches with Emily, so she could have some one-on-one time and support from each. Most important, they did not shame their daughter for her sexual behavior, and they never withheld their love because of her shocking actions.

STAY CURRENT

Once Emily's parents realized how out of touch they were, they worked to become more current in her life. They became involved in school, bringing to light concerns about the atmosphere that contributed to the heavy sexual pressures and activity their daughter had faced. Emily's parents' efforts were transformative, as they used their experiences to help and empower others. Their actions sent a healthy signal to Emily about ways to solve a problem.

SET SMART BOUNDARIES

This Compass point was one Emily's parents used a great deal. Remember, once a boundary is reduced or damaged, it's easier for a person to take advantage and cross it again, or cross the next one—and then a child can find herself on a slippery slope. This was a big concern for Emily's parents. So they talked with her extensively about boundaries, who she could trust, proper ways to explore her feelings, and behaviors that are not appropriate. Most important, they reinforced the idea of Emily's Self Ring and helped her understand her core characteristics, which make up her moral compass. To ensure her continued mental health, her parents arranged for her to have regular check-ins with me.

NURTURE RELATIONSHIPS

Emily joined a sports team at her high school and quickly become one of the best athletes on the team. She was able to form new friendships with her teammates. Participation in sports became a protective factor for her; and she continued to excel. Emily was also able to keep a couple of her oldest and best friends, thanks to outreach from her parents to those girls' parents. In this situation, it was really helpful for Emily to not have to start completely over with new friends, though that's not always possible.

LOSE STIGMA AND PREJUDICE

Emily's parents were careful not to shame their daughter for having been interested in sexuality. Instead of giving in to the discomfort of the situation and trying to just make it go away, her parents explained that it is normal for a person to have sexual feelings and desires. The shock of their daughter's extensive sexual activity allowed them to open up completely, and they were able to emphasize that sex does not equal popularity or love.

All of this contributed to Emily's resilience and got her through the embarrassment, pain, and health implications of her early sexual behavior. Every single person has the ability to develop resilience, however, Emily wasn't accessing the full potential of her inner strength. She always had some resilience within her, but her parents made a concerted effort to build it up to the highest level possible.

Emily was overinfluenced by extrinsic factors—those from the outside, such as popularity. Her parents worked to build up her intrinsic influences—those in her that make up her self-confidence, relationships, and resilience. Since our sessions, Emily has had to continually try to resist extrinsic factors and their effect on her. It's not something she could "get over" easily or quickly, but by being aware of these influences, she was able to create strategies for dealing with them in more positive ways.

Emily's parents also sought support for themselves, which modeled appropriate responses for her but also helped to build their own resilience so they could better care for their daughter. All of these activities, attitudes, and forces converged to buoy Emily through an incredibly risky period and helped her emerge successfully on the other side.

***

All the points on the Parental Compass come together in this final effort: to build your child's resilience in the face of adversity. Resilience has such power that it can propel a person through the turbulence of tragedy and into calmer waters. All our children will face challenges in their lives, and they need to be able to navigate them with as much strength and level-headedness as possible. Drawing upon their resilience allows them to react appropriately and deal with problems effectively. A resilient child can move beyond a difficult situation, learn from a mistake, and know how to avoid it again in the future. The most powerful point on the Parental Compass, resilience allows children to recover from setbacks—even serious ones—and lead happy, healthy lives.

How does your child currently demonstrate resilience?
How will you continue to help them develop it?

_____

_____

_____

_____

_____

_____

_____

_____

_____

_____

_____

_____

_____

_____

_____

_____

_____

_____

_____

_____

_____

_____

_____

_____

CONCLUSION

I have guided parents and children on the subject of sex for nearly two decades, but I have never seen an environment like today's, where so much explicit material is so accessible to so many. The Internet can be great for helping kids learn, staying connected with family and friends who live far away, and keeping up with current events. That powerful force also has a dark side that, despite being filtered or firewalled, is just one click away at any given moment.

The reality is that our kids face many more sexually charged situations than we did as kids. Their landscape now encompasses the pressures of social media and an influx of sexualized images and videos that arrive via their phones. The stories of my patients included in this book personalize the challenges children today may face. Although they are amalgamations of experiences drawn from many children, each conveys the psychological effects that can occur after early or repeated exposure to sexualized content, as well as the harmful results that stigma and prejudice can cause to a child's psyche. Let's make sure their struggles aren't in vain. Honor them by taking lessons from their mistakes. As you work to keep your children safe and help them bounce back from inevitable mistakes, you honor the stories of Sonia, Nathan, Emily, Tyler, and Drew.

The good news is that powerful antidotes to the pressures and problems of growing up—many new, but some ages old—do exist. My Parental Compass offers a crucial navigational tool that you can use to keep your children safe amid these turbulent times. Guided by the principles of the Parental Compass, you can raise strong, resilient kids who, while perhaps not avoiding every pitfall along the way, will be able to circumvent most problems and deal with others as they come up.

What's wonderfully unique about the Parental Compass—and what unites all the stories I've discussed in this book—is that there's no magic formula for perfection, because perfection doesn't exist. Raising strong, resilient children is a project filled with challenges, but the Parental Compass gives you a map by which you can navigate safe passage for you and your family. It guides you to regular practice of principles and strategies that work together to strengthen your bond with your child and boost her resilience in this sexualized, digital world. Take the points that resonate most within your family and capitalize on them in your everyday actions. Remember that parenting is a long game—it's decades made up of years, years made up of days, days made up of moments. Use every moment to enhance your relationship with your child!

THE PARENTAL COMPASS QUICK REFERENCE

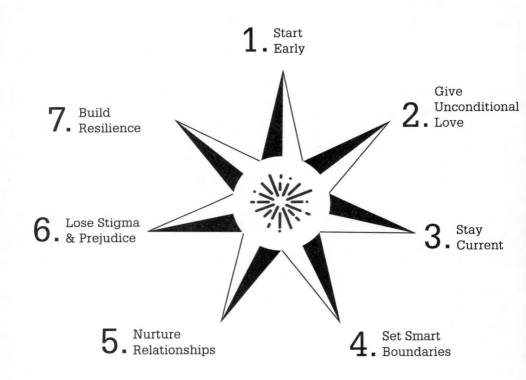

1. Start Early

2. Give Unconditional Love

3. Stay Current

4. Set Smart Boundaries

5. Nurture Relationships

6. Lose Stigma & Prejudice

7. Build Resilience

1. Start Early. An ongoing dialogue with your child throughout her childhood sets you up as the go-to person when she has questions. If she feels safe talking with you as a young child, she'll be more apt to come to you when a serious situation develops, perhaps in her tween or teen years. You need to lose any squeamishness you may feel about discussing sex and sexual topics. Being uncomfortable for a conversation is better than the alternative—that your child will learn about sex from her friends or online.

In addition to the birds and the bees talk, you need to have "The Other Talk," the one where you talk about the kinds of inappropriate content kids may encounter online, how to handle it, and how to avoid it. Explain to your children up front, in a natural, matter-of-fact way, that pornography is not representative of healthy sexual relationships. Make sure to talk with kids throughout their childhood about both healthy sexuality and pornography—children today are seeing more explicit material earlier than children in previous generations.

2. Give Unconditional Love. This advice may sound obvious, but mindful efforts to demonstrate your unwavering love are the best protection you can give to your child. A solid foundation for your parent-child relationship means that you can likely head off some of the challenges of your child's teen years, although that is a rocky time for nearly every family.

3. Stay Current. You need to know what's happening in the world and in your kid's sphere of influence. Monitoring your child's social media use is crucial and does not represent an invasion of your child's privacy. You are your child's biggest influencer, but you must know who else is influencing him. If children see or experience sexual or violent images repeatedly, they can become desensitized, leading to a host of larger problems. Talk with your kids about their interests, and be aware of what they are doing and who they are seeing, both online and off.

4. Set Smart Boundaries. The concept of Concentric Circles—including Self, Family, Community, and Online Rings—illustrates boundaries that protect personal safety as well as instill respect for others. The Concentric Circles help your child see clearly how she relates to the world and how the world *should* relate to her.

5. Nurture Relationships. The biggest threat to our society is the decline in—and possibly absence of—intimacy between two people. Developing good personal social skills and building healthy relationships with friends, classmates, neighbors, and teammates can combat this growing problem. The early relationships your child forms set the stage for him to have healthy relationships as an adult.

6. Lose Stigma and Prejudice. One of the most important things we as parents can model for our children is a positive, inclusive attitude toward people who are different from us. The stigma surrounding the topic of sex needs to go away, and we must learn to discuss issues of sexual orientation and gender identity openly and naturally in our society. Respect and acceptance of diversity can help your child if or when they struggle with their orientation or identity, or if they have a friend who does. Bottom line: You want to focus on the person your child is becoming and leave any preconceived expectations behind. Lose the prejudice and be the caring adult your child needs.

7. Build Resilience. The cumulative point on the Parental Compass, resilience is crucial to your child's healthy development, as resilience and self-confidence are traits that can safeguard him against many negative influences over the long term. Today's challenging landscape demands that we focus on building resilience in our children because, unfortunately, we can't buffer kids from everything. Resilience is like a Teflon coating for your child, allowing him to weather a storm and continue on with life afterward. It's a hardy spirit and strength of character that boosts your child's odds of recovering from adversity. Resilience can be fostered, nurtured, and supported by parents or adult caregivers in a child's life.

RESOURCES

Sexuality Resources

WEBSITES

FamilySparks
www.familysparks.com

CNN Parenting
www.cnn.com/specials/living/cnn-parents

Common Sense Media
www.commonsensemedia.org

Raising Children: Sex Education for Young Children
www.raisingchildren.net.au/articles/sex_education_young_children.html

Advocates for Youth: Helping Parents and Children Talk
www.advocatesforyouth.org/helping-parents-and-children-talk-psec

Kids Health: Talking to Your Kids About Puberty
www.kidshealth.org/en/parents/talk-about-puberty.html

Children Now: Parenting Resources
www.childrennow.org/parenting-resources/sex-relationships

BOOKS

Where Do Babies Come From? Our First Talk About Birth, Dr. Jillian Roberts, Orca Book Publishers, 2015.

What Makes Us Unique? Our First Talk About Diversity, Dr. Jillian Roberts, Orca Book Publishers, 2016.

It's Perfectly Normal: Changing Bodies, Growing Up, Sex, and Sexual Health, Robie H. Harris, Candlewick Press, 2014 (20th anniversary edition).

LGBTQ+ Resources

Egale Canada Human Rights Trust
www.egale.ca

Healthychildren.org: Facts for Teens & Parents
www.healthychildren.org/English/ages-stages/teen/dating-sex/Pages/Gay-Lesbian-and-Bisexual-Teens-Facts-for-Teens-and-Their-Parents.aspx

Stop Bullying: LGBTQ
*www.stopbullying.gov/at-risk/groups/
lgbt*

The Trevor Project
www.thetrevorproject.org

Advocates For Youth
*www.advocatesforyouth.org/topics-
issues/glbtq*

Youth.gov: LGBTQ
*www.youth.gov/youth-topics/lgbtq-
youth*

GLSEN
www.glsen.org

Trans Student Educational Resources
www.transstudent.org

ACKNOWLEDGMENTS

I am so appreciative of my writing partner Sara Au, as well as Dee Ladret, for helping put my vision into words. Thank you to my literary agent Joelle Delbourgo, my editor Erika Heilman, and my developmental editor Susan Lauzau for their roles in making the dream of writing this book a reality. I am also grateful the team at FamilySparks, including my cofounders Rasool Rayani, Dr. Hannes Blum, and Erin Skillen, for all the tremendous assistance they have given me.

The work I do would not be possible without the never-ending support from my family. Stephen, you mean the world to me and I am so grateful to have met you that magical night in 1988. Lauren, you shine and sparkle in so many ways. Ally, you are a pillar of strength and grace. Jack, you light up my heart and give me such joy. I love you all to the moon and back infinity times!

Finally, I am deeply honored by the families who have allowed me to be a partner on their journeys. It has been my life's work to serve you.

ABOUT THE AUTHOR

DR. JILLIAN ROBERTS is a renowned child psychologist, author, professor, and mother. She earned her Ph.D. at age 26, became an associate professor at the University of Victoria at 32, and shortly after became the associate dean of the faculty of education. During this time, Dr. Roberts also built a successful child psychology practice.

Considered a go-to child psychology expert for journalists, Dr. Roberts'

work has appeared in the *New York Times* and the *Toronto Sun*; she is also a regular contributor to the Huffington Post and Global News. Her best-selling and award-winning series of Just Enough children's books explains topics like birth and diversity to children ages 3 to 6 and was released to international acclaim. Her new children's series, The World Around Us, introduces children ages 5 to 8 to issues like poverty and online safety.

In 2017, Dr. Roberts co-founded FamilySparks, a social impact company that offers families timely and supportive resources to help them navigate our increasingly complex world. To learn more, please visit www.familysparks.com or @thefamilysparks on Facebook, Twitter, and Instagram.

Dr. Roberts currently resides in beautiful Victoria, British Columbia, Canada, with her husband Stephen and their three children.

INDEX